# Organizing for Profit in China

# Organizing for Profit in China

## A Case Study Approach

*David S. Wu*

Writers Club Press
New York  Lincoln  Shanghai

Organizing for Profit in China
A Case Study Approach

Writers Club Press
an imprint of iUniverse, Inc.

For information address:
David S. Wu, President
Wu & Associates LLC
dswu@alumni.princeton.edu
http://members.cox.net/wuandassociatesllc

ISBN: 0-595-26796-3

Printed in China

# Dedication

To The Road Warriors:

May successful businesses in China bring you peace and prosperity.

As this book goes to press, my heart goes out to those who may be impacted by SARS (Severe Acute Respiratory Syndrome), the flu-like pneumonia which has claimed too many lives worldwide (including lives of expatriates in China) and closed schools.[1] Fortunately, SARS appears to have peaked already.

*If you want happiness for an hour–take a nap.*
*If you want happiness for a day–go fishing.*
*If you want happiness for a month–get married.*
*If you want happiness for a year–inherit a fortune.*
*If you want happiness for a lifetime–help someone else.*

—*Chinese Proverb*

The following trademarks appear throughout this book: ABB, ALS, AlliedSignal, AmCham, American Motor Company, AMC, Angela Wong & Co., Anheuser Busch, AT&T, Baxter, Bechtel, Bertelsmann, BFGoodrich, Boeing, Booz Allen Hamilton, Cable & Wireless, Carrefour, CCL, Cisco, Character First!, China Eastern Airlines, China Team International, Coca Cola, Cofco, Compaq, Cornerstone International Group, Corning, Craftsman, Danaher, Danaher Business System, DBS, DTM, Deloitte and Touche, Walt Disney, Emerson, Fanta, Fluke, Ford, Fulbright and Jaworski, GE, General Motors, GRE, Haier, Harvard, Healthy Companies International, Hewitt Associates, Hewlett Packard, Honeywell, Hughes, IBM, Jun He, Kentucky Fried Chicken, Kerry, Leadership at the Peak, Legend, Lucent, Maytag, McDonald, MCI, Mercer, Merriam-Webster, Microsoft, Motorola, National Basketball Association, National Geographic, NEC, New York Times, Nike, Nortel, P.L. Thomas & Co., Pepsi, Pope & Associates, Praxair, Princeton, P&T Group, R. R. Donnelley, Rolex, SAT, Schneider Electric, Sears, Shenzhou V, Sidel, Siemens, Sprite, Sun Gazette, Swire, Teligent, Telstra, The Evening Star, TIME, TOEFL, Tyco, USA Today, Vanderbilt, Volkswagen, Wal-Mart, Wang Laboratories, Wharton, Windows, WorldCom, WHO, WTO, Wu & Associates LLC, Xerox, Yale.

# Acknowledgement

In the world of business, China is "The Great Frontier." I address this frontier in what follows, thanks to the tremendous support and guidance received from a broad community. This book presents a glimpse of an imagined utopia and how local and foreign companies are trying to tame the Chinese "frontier." With the community sharing its perspectives, I have been able to offer a broad vision of this frontier.

In this book, Lee Dudka and Sue Jean Lee-Suettinger provided invaluable editorial guidance and comments on the manuscript, especially the Workbook concept and Preface, respectively. Victor Tong, Joyce Greenfield and the iUniverse staff provided production guidance. I would also like to thank YS Chi, Amy Wong and Joe Loughran for their input on the manuscript. Friends from my community also added invaluable comments.

In my career, I would like to thank John Hamilton, Brent Lok, Patricia Pope, Larry Cambron, Larry Bossidy, Fred Poses, Dan Burnham, Tom Johnson, Ken Schwenke, Stephen Rabinowitz, Steven Hochhauser, Bruce Fisher, John Hofmeister, Rob Salek, Bill Davis, Ron Daly, Jim Hsieh, Aki Debayo-Doherty, Clement Mak, Evie Dorman, Frank Poch, Jr., Joe Pugliese, David Burner, Don Barger, Arnold Thaler, Vincent Wan, Jack Todd, David Sweet, John Hayden, Romelle Thompson, Ben Soohoo, Buzz Miller, Alex Zarechnak, Hans Geisecke, Lee Buck, Julian Nichols, Tony Prophet, Pete Walls, and someone I missed. This group taught me the culture to "connect the dots."

As for colleagues in my community, I am most grateful to Dennis and Pollyanna Tsang, George and Betsy Sherman, Frank and Biba Wong, Bob and Shirley Lo, Thomas and Elizabeth Yang, George and Vickie Lee Chu, Ron and Eva Chao, James and Margaret Le, Frankie and Eva Suen, Zhong and Alice Zhang, Anand and Susan Modak, Garry and Bernice Hutchinson, Patrick and Anita Pin, Charles and Julia Wu, Stephen and Amy Kao, Larry and Lynda Cook, Yeqiang and Youying Li Liang, Nai Gang Lu, Zhenhao Li, Wing Ming and Diana Tan, Juliana Mark-Le, Wayne Lau, Kelly and Fumi Kuwayama, Bob Kapp, Iain

McDaniel, Peter and Rebecca Tang, Michael Lam, Philip Chan, Lenka Knowski, Kai Hagan, Mark Williams, Allen Cubell, Derek Johns, Sid Marland, Jan-Pu Hou, Bob Demers, Leigh Shields, Iris Lee, Lucy Zhang, SS Mao, Isabella Zhou, Shirley Li, Stephen Ng, Alex Mark, Andy Rankin, Rosalie Norair, Dan White, Lydia Osborne, Hui-min Tzeng, Vivian Ling, Virginia Moore, Eric van Merkensteijn, William Hamilton, Bill Russel, Dan White, Mike Antal, Bill Schowalter, Eva Lerner-Lam, Helen Zia, Ginny Kamsky, Ellen Rampell, Regina Lee, April Chou, Bill Wong, Mike Podgorny, Leslie Eiser, Miriam Holson, the extended Princeton, Wharton, University of Pennsylvania, Kellogg, Thunderbird, and Center for Creative Leadership communities, and the Greater China Christian communities. My community helped me understand values and patiently taught a naïve entrepreneur everything from faith to life.

Finally, in my life, I am most indebted to my parents, my brother and his wife Jeremy and Deanie Wu, my adopted uncle Bill and aunt Calzina "Cat" Collins-Fletcher, and foremost, my family Elly, Letitia, Lawrence, and Lennifer.

# Comments about

## *"Organizing for Profit in China–A Case Study Approach"*

"This book puts the practical issues into the broader framework of the need for thoughtful and sound management practices and is valuable for business people at all levels of engagement with business in China. Expatriates as the logical vanguard of the new venture and the peculiar dynamics of corporate culture in such a venture are two subjects that receive particularly original and valuable treatment. The book's insights and suggestions have been quite helpful to me in my dealings with China, and I highly recommend this book as a most useful guide and definitive reference text."

—Paul Flowerman, President, P.L. Thomas & Co., Inc.
(International Trade Company Actively Working in China)

"There are well-known ingredients for corporate success. They include skills, knowledge, innovation and ability to manage a company's culture. David S. Wu's book on managing operations in China clearly shows how expatriates can deliver performance. As he shows, culture matters-expatriate managers need the know-how for leading an inclusive workforce abroad. Successful expatriates who learn his guides will be double-blessed for success abroad and at home-since many of his tactics apply equally well in managing diverse workforces in the US."

—Patricia C. Pope, CEO, Pope & Associates, Inc.
(Pope Inclusion Network diversity consultants since 1976)

"…case studies (in this book) provide the much needed empirical foundation for China business and investment currently lacking from the available literature. I strongly recommend this as reading for business professionals as well as investment advisors, lawyers and others with a serious interest in understanding the complex mechanics of the China market."

—Tibor Baranski, Counsel, Jun He Law Offices (Beijing)

"…The book takes us through the culture building path which is essential to the long term success of building a profitable company in China…"

—Dr. Brent Lok, President, Praxair China

"…(written by) a superior manager who knows how to deal with business and people in China. His abundant knowledge based on his experience in China and other Asian countries provide great help to the readers."

—Jason KH Lee, Human Resources Director, Cisco Systems–Asia Pac

"I recommend this book for anyone interested in doing business in China. The insights shared in this book can only come from someone who has experienced the challenges of business development within China. This book addresses some of the factors often overlooked when attempting to expand a company's presence in China."

—Lawrence D. Cook, Director of Materials, Maytag Corporation, Cleveland Cooking Products Division

"…Having the right products and services…and having the right people are the keys to success in any business venture, especially in China…(the author) addresses these important elements with in-depth analysis supported by real life examples. A great book for readers who want to be successful in China's business world."

—Stephen Kao, Vice President Asia Pacific, Emerson Process Management

"This book doesn't exaggerate nor sensationalize. It serves as a practical guide for helping readers understand China and how to be profitable rather than just being another company trying to stay in business…Great book."

—Charles Wu, General Manager, Software Group, IBM Greater China

"…the reader…benefits greatly from (the author's) experiences in doing business in China."

**—Jenni Smith, General Manager, Human Resources, Telstra Int'l**

"…great book containing real experiences and points for profit…"

**—George Chu, Vice President, Coca Cola-China (Retired)**

"…fascinating real life experiences in China…book is a great guide to the opportunities and pitfalls to be expected as an expatriate in Asia. It is an excellent guide and testimony to life abroad…"

**—Jeffrey Blount, Fulbright and Jaworski (Hong Kong)**

"…with many years of experience behind him in China business and South East Asia, the author helps readers save lots of time in finding questions they may not know to ask but must ask if they want success in doing business in China…"

**—Dennis Tsang, Director, P & T Group (Hong Kong)**

"This book has…real life accountabilities of business culture in China. Reading this book will save time and money for the readers…with existing Chinese operations and those seeking opportunities in China."

**—Frank Wong, former Deputy President, Baxter Healthcare China**

"…a valuable guide to delivering sustained profitable growth for products and services in China."

**—Ralph I. Miller, China Business Consultant, Media and Telecommunications**

"China…in 21st century is like England in the 19th century and US in the 20th century. Shanghai is becoming the commercial epicenter like Lancashire and Detroit…(the book is) thoroughly researched and presented in an easy-to-read format. This is a must read book for anyone doing business in China, either as an entrepreneur or as an expatriate."

**—Gordon Hau, Vice President, ABB China**

*Do not follow where the path may lead.*
*Go, instead, where there is no path and leave a trail.*

*—Ralph Waldo Emerson*

# Preface

Nearly a decade ago, I became an expatriate manager for AlliedSignal (now Honeywell) in China. It drew me into a world from which I still draw lessons. I went abroad to use my skills in a new environment, and to create steppingstones to new opportunities back home in the US. My children were young, and I knew I'd return when they were ready for high school.

Today, my children are in American schools, my family lives in Virginia, and I've now turned to helping future "expats" get a good start in Asia. In between, I held off returning from China because new opportunities proliferated.

I switched jobs in Asia, continued to succeed, and regularly had people offering me new options. Given those successes, I thought that most companies, when needed, would repatriate me into new "slots," especially since I continually delivered results.

Then, my surprise: The more I broached repatriation, the more I saw that it's relatively rare to navigate it successfully. Success overseas does not translate into options at home, at commensurate ranks in the US.

The conclusion dawned on me only slowly. Expatriate assignments are tough on the "back end," when you're ready to go "home."

Some of my "road warrior" friends love living in China. I love something else: I'm a Washingtonian at heart and prefer life in the US. Life overseas also incurs costs. As an expatriate abroad, you grow your overseas network, but you watch your "home-based" version shrink. Still, success is its own motivator, and I had it: Setting up AlliedSignal's one profitable investment in China, launching the first million-dollar sales initiative for Danaher Instrument and Controls, creating still more innovations or managing ongoing operations for top-echelon US companies. Despite my success, I missed that intriguing reward in the end, a chance for a "step up" in the US. So I'm now helping others ensure a smoother ride back as "expats."

There is one major dimension to this. As a key high-ranking Asian American during my expatriate years, I still faced hurdles identifying effective mentors, from any level of senior management. Fellow executives at home, I know, are thriving through mentoring.

So mentoring is clearly one solution here. The right pointers on how to "promote" yourself, connect with important senior executives, and get advice for handling internal politics–all these are critical to any future expatriate.

**Hence, this book: It's dedicated to the thousands of fellow road warriors who've shared my experience and my journey. And to the new ones like you, dear reader**, who know you'll succeed despite the challenge ahead.

For now, I offer the fruits of my learning in my nearly decade-long "journey to Asia." In addition, **this book specifically highlights the best of my "lessons learned"** in Asian start-ups and ongoing operations. It helps you launch your planning for your Asian tour of duty, prepares you for the big hurdles, and offers my lessons drawn from similar situations.

One lesson I offer US-based global companies: You need better career progression for expatriates coming "home." In a global economy, you need quality-controlled processes so that **successful expatriate talent–your best candidates for future assignments** in many ways–gets short-listed for work in the US. As a business process reengineering (BPR) professional, I'd say this is your next BPR process target.

Don't just take my word for this. Listen to C. William Guy, Chairman and CEO of the Cornerstone International Group, the world's largest human capital consortium. He offers a "twist of the thinking cap":

> "Post-assignments of expatriates ('repatriation') should be in each successful company's employee benefit program. *What is needed is for global companies to manage and publicize the repatriations of their successful expatriates [italics added]*. Otherwise, the expatriates are not motivated to deliver results–they become "career" expatriates-and their employers fail to localize company competencies. Hence, multi-national companies are wasting millions on such hidden costs and lost opportunities to gain an edge on their competitors."

This book, then, reflects a firsthand view of the issues that expatriate managers face, in running daily operations, and in planning long-term about career progression.

By sharing my lessons learned, I'm happy to support the many corporate managers who recruit and deploy talented staff overseas. Successful expatriate managers are both tough and realistic: They want to and will achieve—no matter what obstacles they encounter in foreign environments.

One thing is certain: Guide and support your expatriates, and they'll be your top leaders and mentors, capably handling all of your China-based staffers. They'll create nimble operations in China, and build profitable businesses that you'll be proud to nurture.

*David S. Wu*

*April, 2003*

# Snapshot of China's Place in Our World

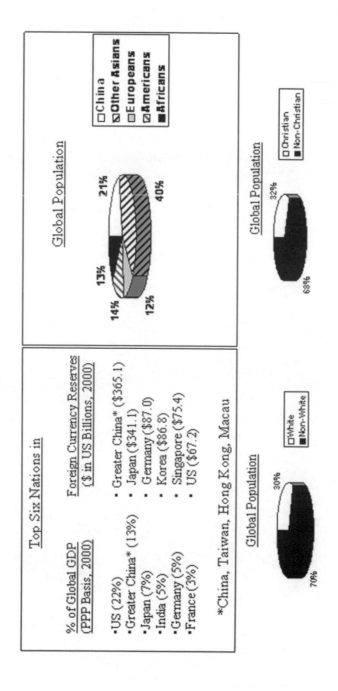

## Top Six Nations in

### % of Global GDP
(PPP Basis, 2000)

- US (22%)
- Greater China* (13%)
- Japan (7%)
- India (5%)
- Germany (5%)
- France (3%)

### Foreign Currency Reserves
($ in US Billions, 2000)

- Greater China* ($365.1)
- Japan ($341.1)
- Germany ($87.0)
- Korea ($86.8)
- Singapore ($75.4)
- US ($67.2)

*China, Taiwan, Hong Kong, Macau

### Global Population

30%
70%

□ White
■ Non-White

### Global Population

21%
13%
14%
12%
40%

□ China
▨ Other Asians
□ Europeans
▧ Americans
■ Africans

### Global Population

32%
68%

□ Christian
■ Non-Christian

Sources:  See Footnotes 2, 3, 4, and 5 of this book and Wu & Associates LLC.  Some statistics are subject to interpretations.
For detailed statistics, see http://www.prb.org/pdf/WorldPopulationDS02_Eng.pdf.

*It is by chance we met,*
*by choice we became friends.*

*—Unknown*

# About the reader

**The use of the word "you" in this book primarily refers to the business managers responsible for delivering profit in China.** You are the senior executives of the 42 million enterprises[6] in US, Europe and Australia working in Human Resources, Legal, Finance, Logistics, Sales, Marketing, Corporate Development, Operations, Engineering, Purchasing, Trading, etc. Collectively, you are responsible for:

- Delivering profit on US$40-70 billion/year Foreign Direct Investment in China[7]
  - 25,000 non-Chinese funded enterprises[50]
  - US$300 billion sales[50]
  - 6 million employees[50]
- US$30-50 billion/year expenses for the expatriates[21]
- US$500 billion/year total import and export trades[50]

Most of you are attracted by the enormous market and low cost supplier potential in China, especially after China's entry into the World Trade Organization and with the 2008 Beijing Olympics. Many of you have traveled to China looking for an entry point to conduct business or have some local representation in China for your products and services. Some of you already have expatriates based in China or you are an expatriate supervising local staff, and a few of you are already established in China, with local Chinese managers sustaining your business growth.

You know you have a winner, but your team is not where you think they should be. You are willing to make investments to generate profit, but your vignettes of doing business in China are not always pleasant. For you, you will use the concepts in this book to create your own "30 Minute Workbook" and find out where you should focus your efforts and have the biggest impact on your China operation.

**For training institutes** (especially ones that focus on diversity training), this book focuses on expatriates who must be culturally sensitive leaders and drive an inclusive workforce in order to deliver performance. Global diversity must be driven by business performance which is the target of existing diversity initiatives in the US.

**For students of international business,** the case studies in this book are written in the style taught at top MBA schools around the world. The epilogues will enhance the learning experience.

Finally, **for families of current or prospective expatriates**, you can get a glimpse of the work-life balance issues of living aboard. Families of expatriates can be more prepared for the everyday challenges in a country that is culturally very different. This will reduce the anxiety of planning and/or making the transition to living in China.

*When ice is three feet thick,*
*It is not due to coldness of one day.*

*—Chinese Proverb*

# Engaging your counterparts

**The bumper sticker says, "Think global, act local." It's not that easy.**

If you're engaging the "globally-minded" Chinese, you need an awareness of China's place in the world. And there's much to learn about their history, people and culture if you want familiarity with China's complex environment before you "hit the ground" for meetings.

Your goal is to set up profitable business in China, but first things first: **Learn to listen to, and engage your Chinese counterparts**. Creating strategy and tactics, selecting personnel–all that's for later, and we'll cover it in depth in these pages.

**Start by getting prepared**. One model is Honeywell's Larry Bossidy as he courted Chinese counterparts throughout China. He prepared Chinese "talking points."

And Bossidy succeeded. He could navigate conversations because he studiously did his homework. You can do the same, using samples like the one below on intellectual property, a "burning issue" in China. (For an array of *"Talking point starters,"* please see the *Appendix*.)

Review it, and consider these additional guides:

- Stay open-minded to learning even more from your Chinese hosts, and
- Develop your own perspectives on "China topics" critical to your business.

   **Talking Point Sample: Protection of intellectual property**–a major point of frustration in China. It's frustrating to think that, as you enter China for business, you have a bigger chance of losing your intellectual property than you do of striking a deal.

   Why? The Chinese government is working hard to establish a legal framework within the global community, but there are limits to its powers. For enforcement of its policies, it has 66 million Chinese Communist Party members (2002 figures), but that reflects but 5% of the country's population–1 in 20 Chinese.

What are the other hurdles? The biggest is the lack of a collective will to obey "global" laws. The Chinese need to collectively **want to comply** with foreign (and now domestic) laws and regulations.

What's the roadmap for getting there? One Chinese historical vignette can help.

Beginning in early 1800's and continuing for over a century, foreign nations (the US, Britain, Germany, France, Russia, Japan, Spain, and Italy) entered China with impunity. They brought gunboats, and often showed no respect for the people with whom they conducted their business. Opium was introduced mostly by the British in the early 19th century and had a devastating effect on the large mass of people coaxed into its addictive use. Circa World War II, there were signs near Shanghai's Bund park warning that "Dogs and Chinese not allowed." (Picture a parallel scene in New York City's Central Park, with signs saying, "Dogs and Americans not allowed.") To Chinese eyes, such condescension sparked the view that "foreign devils" can't be trusted.

As you share your views, your hosts will share theirs. Creating an atmosphere of openness and willingness to engage will facilitate building mutual trust. And you give "face" to the Chinese as you look for "common ground." The trick with common ground: Find it, then sit back and listen. You engage as you listen, and learn "the lay of the land."

**Your goal and ours is to develop your profitable business**. To help you on your journey, we offer additional "*talking point starters*" in the *Appendix*–all linked to the history that's been a staple of discussions at Chinese meetings during my 8 years in China.

Remember to give these "*talking point starters*" the proper context when you prepare your "*talking points*" in China

**By doing your homework like Larry Bossidy, you'll be truly equipped to learn from your many Chinese counterparts sitting right across the table from you.**

\*                    \*                    \*

*Books are the quietest and most constant of friends;*
*they are the most accessible and wisest of counsellors,*
*and the most patient of teachers.*

*—Charles W. Eliot (1834–1926)*

# Table of Contents

*One picture is worth ten thousand words.*

*—early 20th century English Proverb*

# List of Illustrations

**Chapter 1**

**Chapter 2**

**Section II**

**Chapter 4**

**Chapter 9**

**Case #1**

*Begin with the end in mind.*

*---Habit #2, **Seven Habits of Highly Effective People***
*Stephen Covey*

# Section I

# Overview

You're a successful company, but you also want to succeed in China. Or, you're there already, but you need a good roadmap for expanding and doing brisk business.

Bookstores are crammed with books that will help you sort out the many parts of the Chinese business landscape, but this one is a bit different.

This book is designed to help you profit in China, right from the start, using an evolving, continually improving process that accelerates your growth and reduces your costs. To take your best shot at this, you will be asked to do a serious self-assessment–one that pinpoints where to focus in your China operations, so that your strategies get the biggest "bang for the buck."

**What will this mean for you?**

This book offers a time-tested process that will grow your China-based business. Five case studies support your effort to implement this process.

**This book's key premises:**

- **You're ready to develop a global culture** based on your key competencies and competitive strengths.
- **You will dedicate key expatriates** as "ambassadors" to China, and lead them in their effort to localize your company's strengths–aided by trained local Chinese managers.

1

- **You can designate and train local managers** who will customize your company's strengths to fit local market conditions.

Your process will focus on

- A clear understanding of your goals for China operations.
- Your expatriates' skill in handling Chinese culture and successfully coaching local managers to grow the China business.
- Your Chinese managers' skills in adapting a healthy culture and strong character as they customize your organization's strengths to local market conditions.

The outcome: Your company really will have a process that **"thinks globally, acts locally."** With it, you will establish a global culture, but manage it locally. And you will succeed–provided you establish an effective, healthy culture and what we call "strong character" in China.

As you implement this process, and target continuous improvement, you will want to zero in on the weakest point of your operations.

**What is the weakest point in creating China-based operations?** From discussions with many successful expatriates in China (reflecting many industries), we know one overwhelming weakness in many operations: The ability to motivate expats and develop local managers to replace them.

This point is weak for a reason. That is, "localization" slows considerably whenever your expatriates are kept in the dark about their future career path–the path **after** their China-based assignments.

This is no surprise. "Expats" in China usually lack "next-step" career plans. **Typical China-based assignments are off the track** for future career success, so motivating expats becomes a "tough sell." What's more, if your expats lack a vision of their future, and clear-cut motivation for moving ahead, your teams can't deliver superior results.

Many factors are behind this. For one thing, China assignments are "unbundled" from successful career paths because of the small size of the business. For another, there are few senior managers paying attention and nurturing the business *and* the expatriate talent. Yet both need attention.

On the management side, senior managers fail to nurture China businesses because they themselves lack direction, but they also lack the know-how. This book shows them where to begin, and how to sustain that nurturing process so it benefits the business and the loyal expatriates running it.

If these points ring true to you–as a senior manager in a home office, a soon-to-be expatriate, or a local manager in China–you're ready for the action oriented strategy found in these pages. Your first step: Establish what your company can do in China, then pick expatriates who can deliver what you need done.

And, ensure your expatriates have a future career track once they accept their China "duty tours." Then, "walk the talk." Make the point convincingly by championing successful repatriations in all of your company-wide messages.

How will this benefit you? Successful repatriation means something else has succeeded: the development of local managers. Don't define success as expatriates changing assignments. Hold the expats responsible for longer periods–until your China operation actually delivers bigger profit.

Do this, and you'll start to see superior talent competing for China assignments. You'll see improvements in your bottom line and company morale at home and abroad. You've got nothing to lose but old, hit-and-miss ways of driving your business. What are you waiting for? *Read on.*

# Section by Section Orientation

This book is divided into five sections and is designed to help you achieve more profits, at a faster rate, by directing your attention to these areas:

Section I: What are your goals for profitable growth in China? This section

- Establishes a 6-phase Business Life Cycle for sustained growth
- Introduces the concept of global diversity as an extension of (North American) diversity training
- Differentiates the separate processes of seeking low cost suppliers, versus trying to sell in China
- Illustrates the key steps for establishing sustainable competitive advantage

Target audience: Businesses either beginning to explore the China market, traveling to China, or exporting and importing from China.

Section II: How do you achieve your goals through expatriates? This segment helps you reach your goals by

- Introducing a Career Life Cycle concept for "growth driver" leaders
- Describing the framework and key selection criteria for setting up your overseas expatriates
- Identifying key features in compensation and work-life balance issues for your expatriates

5

- Recommending overseas assignments as vital employee development paths to future career growth

**Target audience:** Expatriates and supervisors working in businesses with at least one Representative Office already in China (or about to be launched there), and looking to deliver profits and build the management team.

**Section III: How do you achieve your goals through a strong operational culture and "company character"?** This section

- Establishes one key idea: Healthy company cultures with "strong character" deliver profitable growth
- Identifies ways to motivate local employees after expatriates repatriate "home" (and assume the next steps in a structured career track)
- Shows how Taiwan and Hong Kong expatriates can contribute to Greater China businesses and identifies their special development needs

**Target audience:** Any product or service company committed to making China its long-term global market and trying to get more from its expatriate team "on the ground."

**Section IV: How do you customize this book for your China operations?**

- Complete our extensive Workbook and seriously target those operational areas that demand improvement.
- Focus on creating targeted initiatives to deliver sustained profitable growth. Do so by integrating two key concepts in this book, the Business and Career Life Cycles, and capturing their value through higher productivity.

**Finally, Section V presents five case studies with epilogues** similar to the way top MBA schools in the world use case studies to illustrate operational issues. A summary of Case Study #3–ASH

Conglomerate, is presented on p. 42 for your reference. Collectively, they bring the concepts in this book to life for you.

**Note**

*Before anything else, preparation is the key to success.*

*—Alexander Graham Bell*

# Chapter 1

# Establishing our framework

## *Executive Summary*

- *China's **market potential is enormous** and your business can benefit from **recently lowered risks** of setting up in China as China begins to conform to WTO's international trade rules.*

- *Expatriates drive overseas growth, but the aggregate cost is US$30-50 billion annually. As you will soon see, your mastery of **Phases 4-6 of the "Business Life Cycle"** gives you a framework for actively **accelerating your business growth** in China.*

- *As you prepare to deploy your expatriates, you will discover—by "polling" their ideas—that **they succeed to the degree they are successful managers of diverse teams** in the US.*

**Fast Facts**

**Who are your competitors** for China-based business?

Let's start with the "big picture" that includes competitors and more: Over 15 million corporations and partnerships with employees, plus 27 million sole proprietorships, or 42 million total business enterprises in the US, Europe and Australia.[6] Many want opportunities in the enormous Greater China market (i.e., China, Taiwan, Hong Kong, and Macau).

9

Lots of competition, but also lots of opportunity.

Why is that? Greater China has the highest foreign currency reserves in the world today.[4] China alone received an estimated US$50 billion Foreign Direct Investment in 2002,[7] an estimate that topped the US's for the first time, making China the most attractive place to invest. As of 1993, China was recognized as having the second-largest economy when measured by the International Monetary Fund[8] purchasing power parity (PPP) approach. With 8% annual growth in the 1990s[9] during a global recession and an Asian currency crisis, China sparks the idea that the "21st century belongs to Asia."[10] China (and Taiwan) joined the WTO in December 2001, after winning the bid for the 2008 Olympics in Beijing.

**In fact, nothing competes with China as an attractive market.** Compared to the US, China has a bigger land mass and over 400% more people. Already, China is the world's largest market for cellular phones and color television sets, yet the penetration rate is still relatively low compared to the overall population. In the 1990s, the most popular picture of cranes in China is not of a picturesque bird, but of metal-clad building cranes. About 10% of the banks' outstanding loans in China, or US$150 billion, are tied up in real estate. After China's 1998 decision to begin eliminating free and subsidized housing, US$95 billion flooded into real estate in 2002 alone.[11] Also in 2002, Kentucky Fried Chicken had over 700 outlets in China and was averaging one new outlet every other day.[12]

But there's more. IBM, Compaq, and the local Legend personal computers compete to support the country's quickly spiking Internet needs. NEC and Taiwanese semiconductor companies are building multi-billion-dollar wafer fabrication facilities in eastern China. China sells over 1 million cars at home as its steadily rising middle class continues to emerge.[13] Ford and GM, two of the top three global car companies, demand that their global parts suppliers be from China, driving a major structural shift in the supply chain and related logistics from other geographies to China. China will also become the world's largest shipbuilder once Korea moves some of its capabilities to China. On December 31, 2002, China demonstrated the world's first commercial Magnetic Levitation Train in Shanghai that traveled at a peak speed of 260 miles per hour on a 14-mile, 19-minute journey at an expense of US$1.2 billion,[14] and there are projections of a Shenzhou V Manned Space Mission in the near future.[15]

## The promise

To reiterate: You'll find the most promising Chinese business sectors to reflect a wide range of industries:

- Automobile production and parts
- Building materials and systems
- Cellular phones and consumer appliances
- Fast-moving consumer goods
- Logistics and distribution
- Mass transit systems
- Personal computers
- Semiconductors
- Shipbuilding
- Space technologies

You can even establish connections among the ranks of Chinese entrepreneurs. Chinese companies are becoming known for their entrepreneurs and successful Chinese brands such as Haier.[16] For the first time in 2002, the Chinese government acknowledged the contribution of its private enterprises to the development of the economy. Huawei, a 1988 Chinese startup, now successfully produces and sells network routers and switches, and in 2001, earned US$578 million on US$2.4 billion sales. It boasts distributors in Germany and Great Britain and new sales offices in northern Virginia, San Jose (California), and Dallas, Texas.[17]

Lots of promise in a promising market—but how do **you** make money in the midst of such promise?

Despite encouraging signs of promise, not all foreign businesses can compete successfully in China. In fact, US and European companies find profit elusive even after making major investments.

Siemens and ABB, with decades of investment in China's infrastructure projects, are patiently awaiting their return on investment. Pepsi, despite over US$500 million invested in China, still cannot compete with Coca Cola,[18] while the domestic Chinese brands are competing with both Coca Cola and Pepsi.

### Success factors

This is the open secret about China: Just as its local entrepreneurs succeed, so can you. You need a large measure of patience, and you need something else. An old bit of Chinese wisdom goes, "**Thirty percent of business is waiting.**" In today's Chinese economy, we insist that you also need "**intelligent waiting**" to succeed.

So try to practice patience while we take you through the smart steps you need to succeed.

### First steps: Your 3 Ps of Risk

You probably evaluate business prospects with a business projection, so let's start with that. Small businesses use such projections in simplified format–or they might not even commit them to writing. At minimum, you surely have a picture in mind of taking more money out than you bring into China, after accounting for costs. This is your return on investment. Business projections are useful tools to facilitate approvals within your company. Some companies look at the business projection over 3 years, some over 5 or even 10 years. The Japanese are known to look at business projections as long as 150 years into the future.

A question: **How much return is right for you?** To answer this question, quantify your risks. Also include investments that require other people to help you execute. Use one premise: You alone can not accomplish as much as a team can accomplish by working with you.

Shift focus, now, to investments that require a team to execute. Since no one thinks and executes exactly as you do, you must provide a framework to help others focus on working with you and delivering results. You also need a process to help others know how you make decisions, or else it's pot luck whether your stateside successes can be duplicated in China.

In short, we've just described the "**3 P's of risk**":

- **Project risk**–selecting your projects or investments
- **People risk**–focusing your team on delivering results, and
- **Process risk**–managing your culture and character

Before we discuss these risks in much greater detail, let's establish how you can quantify your risks in order to help you evaluate your business projections.

**Two approaches to quantifying risk:**

Since an inflation-impacted dollar tomorrow is not worth the same as a dollar today, financial managers chart the streams of cash inflow and outflow with a single value. They decide how much to discount that future dollar into "present value." Two popular ways to "discount" future dollars are:

- **Find the Internal Rate of Return**–Estimate the equivalent profit rate at zero present value after accounting for the dollar investments. This yields a percentage figure we call the *Internal Rate of Return*.
- **Find the Net Present Value**–Use a risk-adjusted cost of capital to discount future cash flow and show the opportunity cost of the investment dollar amount. This yields a dollar figure, the so-called *Net Present Value*.

Many financial texts give you the advantages and disadvantages of both methods. For our purposes, the key is this: **Higher-risk investments mean greater expectations of profit**. To capture this risk, the financial community created an elegant parameter called a "beta"[19]–where 1.0 is the generally accepted risk for a typical company. Higher risks, measured by a beta over 1.0, bring higher expectations of profit or greater return on investment.

Let's check the *beta* for your potential risks in China. Until 2002, China operations carried a high risk premium. Reason: As an emerging economy, it wasn't compliant with international standards of trade. But once it entered the WTO (2001), its risk premium began dropping and the justification for Chinese investments became easier. Notice, however: If your team handling China business lacks experience, you should reflect this lack of experience in risk assessments for investment justifications.

**A visa example:** US citizens need a visa to enter China. US expatriates must have work permits, residency permits, and health certifications before expatriate visas (Type "Z") can be issued.

So if you are visiting China, here are your three options:

- OPTION 1: Typically, you must have a business visa after receiving an invitation letter from a legal representative of a recognized Chinese enterprise. You submit this letter, your visa application, fees and your passport to the Chinese embassy or consulate before your visa can be issued (7-10 days). Note: The process will require some advanced planning for you.

- OPTION 2: You can travel to Hong Kong, where an entry visa is not needed, then get your China visa while you're there. Most Hong Kong travel agents issue valid Chinese visas within 24 hours–no need for an invitation letter.

- OPTION 3: With some airlines that let you fly without a visa, you can get your visa on arrival at the Chinese airport. You run a risk: You may not be allowed to enter if you're not approved.

Choose wisely. But to illustrate the idea of beta with getting a visa: Your beta is the standard 1.0 if you travel to Hong Kong for your visa. But your beta is less than 1.0 if you opt to request an invitation letter first. And your beta is higher than 1.0 if you decide to go to China first and try getting your visa at the airport.

### Growth Risks and Profits

How do you size up profitable growth potential? Your best bet: View this through the lens of the *"Business Life Cycle"* (shown in Exhibit 1-1). The concept is taught in business schools throughout the world. The "Business Life Cycle" (BLC) is based on one core idea, the "core competency."

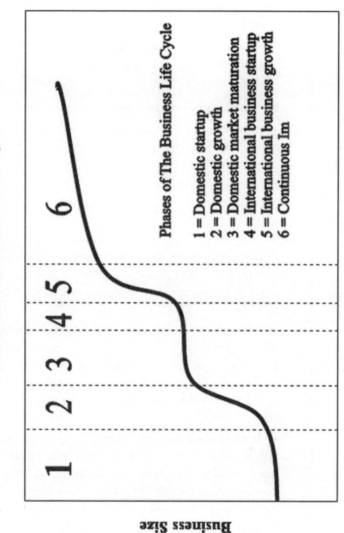

Exhibit 1-1
Six Phases of The Business Life Cycle

Phases of The Business Life Cycle

1 = Domestic startup
2 = Domestic growth
3 = Domestic market maturation
4 = International business startup
5 = International business growth
6 = Continuous Im

Business Size

Time

Note

We define **core competency** this way: It is your business skill that *goes beyond* your capabilities, but it produces high-level results about 90% of the time. Example: Wal-Mart invested US$1 billion in its inventory control system in the 1990s, and it now boasts a competency in inventory systems that's second to none.[20]

Try this way of seeing **your core competency**: It's the **magnet** that attracts your key customers, either in the US or in China.

As for the BLC's individual phases:

**The Business Life Cycle's 6 Phases–where success in business tracks a serpentine curve that slowly rises (*see* next page):**

**1- Domestic market startup.** In the initial phase, the "whiff" of competition sharpens your skills to deliver local customer satisfaction. If yours is a US business, this means the US market.

**2- Domestic market grows.** Key customers accept your product (or service), and growth accelerates as more core competencies emerge–you learn to provide a benefit and beat competitors at it.

**3- Domestic profitable growth slows.** Cost, new technology and competition begin to slow down your growth. Businesses typically try to shift their core competencies into related areas, e.g, to the domestic market. Strategic teams test the idea that your company's core competency can be translated overseas.

**4- International business startup.** This phase starts as you export components of your core domestic business. And you face a hurdle: Your techniques for sizing up profitable markets like China's are usually hard to apply because the validating data is either expensive or unavailable.

**5- International business grows.** As attractive foreign markets are found, you try to reach more customers or reduce the costs of delivering your product to customers. You try to detect the cost benefits of investing in a foreign site. Soon, you identify local products with local characteristics.

**6- Continuous improvements sustain the business life cycle.** Without international business or continuous improvement, many businesses die prematurely. Timing and ability to adapt are critical. *Example*: The once-dominant Wang Laboratories word processing machines, a business that failed to continuously improve. Since Wang failed to make Wang word processors compatible with emerging software like Microsoft Windows, customers simply switched to WordPerfect or Microsoft Word as other Windows-based personal computers came on the market. Result: A flourishing business died. Now, post-baby-boom generations have not even heard of Dr. An Wang, founder of Wang Laboratories, philanthropist and US computer pioneer.

**Why focus on phases 4-6** of the Business Life Cycle? They help you to

- Reduce costs and shorten startup time in your China business (Phase 4).

- Maximize the growth of your China business (Phase 5).

- Increase the growth rate of continuous improvement (Phase 6) in your evolving business cycle for China-based operations.

Think seriously about how this cycle works in your business. First, **how do you reduce startup cost and time**? In Phase 4, you'll do this by acquainting yourself with your customers and using the right expatriate team. In turn, you will maximize growth (Phase 5) by successfully "transitioning" from an expatriate team to local team management of your operations. This drives new features and benefits after localizing your products or services. Finally, as you increase your growth rate (Phase 6) via continuous improvements, your pace will depend, in large measure, both on the culture of your expatriate "players" and your local management teams.

Consider each of these **3 crucial phases** in greater detail.

**Phase 4: Reduce cost and shorten startup time in your China business**

It costs US$350,000 annually for each expatriate senior manager you send (see *Chapter 4*). All told, there are an estimated 100,000 to 200,000 expatriates in China[21]. (At its peak, Lucent Technologies spent several hundred million dollars annually supporting its 1,200 expatriates in China.) Overall, this means companies spend US$30-50 billion every year for their expatriates. With such high expenses, it may surprise you to learn that many employees go overseas because they have no choice about the assignment, or they choose it eventually to retire overseas.

In short, bad reasons often drive employee teams to China. So what are the **good reasons**? The good news is that you **can make the right choices** and cost effectively achieve your globalization mission.

But you must study the processes used by companies with a successful track record in China—using their tools, along with "smart waiting" to create a solid operations "platform" for your team. More on this below, but let's move to the decision points you face right now.

Let's assume you already have a "China-ready" US company. We then need to **pinpoint your attributes** that deliver success here in the US. Next, we move to evaluate whether those attributes are "translatable" to Greater China. Most companies are beyond "version 1.0" of this step at this point, especially since China opened her doors in 1978. Usually, an advance team—based on your company's experience, outside consultants, or market research—helps establish the framework for market entry in China. We will quickly move to identify and develop your attributes (whether costs, technology, processes), and do so in *Chapter 3*.

But for the moment, let's dwell on the first iteration of this step because you have 2 teams to satisfy: your business development and your operations teams. Each has different needs. Each relies on different information and different information sources. To cite Ron Chao, Deloitte and Touche partner based in Shanghai: **"You face many pitfalls, and substantial loss of investments in Greater China, from one discontinuity**—and that's the gap between your first steps and your later monitoring of your business development."

How does any company guard against this "discontinuity"? Better put, **how do you maintain continuity** between your initial planning and what you're doing once you're operating in China?

First, review your assumptions justifying your China investment. It's fanciful (but impractical) to believe you'll maintain such continuity through management changes, and not adjust your expectations along the way. But these changes must remain consistent with your company policy guidelines regarding resource allocation and investment decisions.

Remember, too, the vital role of people, your "expat team." Companies are inanimate entities, despite how tax authorities treat them. So your success or failure is dictated by people and sustained through an evolving culture you develop consciously over time. The company culture (defined by you and senior managers) impacts your ability to recruit and motivate expatriate employees critical to your first day of overseas operations. To consistently drive profits, you must reward employees who deliver your core competencies overseas to overseas customers. Do this, and you will retain a group of loyal, high-value employees with overseas experience. And you will cut costs usually linked to long expatriate assignments, employee turnover, and related recruitment and training expenses.

**Phase 5: Maximize the growth of your China business**

Who maximizes the growth of your China business? It's your team of expat and local managers who repackage your product's benefits to meet unique customer requirements in China. To do this, your expatriates must

- **Behave as leaders** who understand, communicate, and support the key growth attributes for overseas business. Remember: They are your ambassadors offering your core competencies overseas.

- **Stay aware of cultural differences** in the local work environment. They must be able to grasp the product (or service) attributes needed to adapt locally and succeed.

- **Manage an inclusive workforce** that can motivate and develop local talent. Your expatriate managers are unlikely to know the local culture better than the local employees. So expatriates can succeed only when local employees are developed.

- **Deliver performance.** Given the high cost of expatriates (noted earlier), your business will see rising profitability as your expatriate assignment tours are shortened.

These four characteristics, coincidentally, are well known within the training and leadership development circles as the actual focus of diversity training. Exhibit 1-2 shows "Diversity's Four Elements" at AlliedSignal (now Honeywell)[22] as early as 1994.

You will not be able to deliver profit overseas if you are culturally insensitive and cannot manage an inclusive workforce.

This raises an obvious question: Can diversity training tools be extended to international business? By now, it's clear that the answer is "yes."

The key to extending your diversity focus to international business is making an effective transition from expatriate management to local management. So you will not only recruit a diverse workforce, you will depend on it to perform after you are gone. In global diversity terms, you cross a major threshold once you step back from your international business role, and your local managers take over. This is when your company begins to enjoy true success.

**Phase 6: Increase the growth rate of continuous improvement in your Business Life Cycle (Phase 6)**

We've seen how overseas business can reinforce and strengthen your home office commitment to continuous improvement. So, establish a team of diverse, "global-business-ready" leaders, and you have your foundation for remaining on top of your competition.

This is especially true in China where intellectual property rights, at times, are not strictly enforced. Depending on your operations, the performance (and survival) of your China-based business depend on continuous improvement.

## Exhibit 1-2
## Diversity Characteristics Adopted by AlliedSignal (Honeywell)

**Leadership**

Everyone needs to understand and support what diversity is. We need to talk about it and communicate what we mean by it. We need to find role models and champions of it.

**Awareness**

Education and training throughout our businesses will create greater sensitivity to the issue. We'll take a proactive approach to air and resolve problems at all levels of our organization. Everyone will receive some kind of orientation to diversity by the end of 1995.

**Reinforcement**

Our systems and processes will become stronger to support our diversity strategy. For example, we need to determine what our company policy is on work/life issues and adapt it at the business/site/local levels so that employees can empower themselves to be more productive. We need to retain and recruit employees who reflect a diverse workforce.

**Performance**

We need to monitor our results, from the Employee Satisfaction Survey and other evaluations, to closely review the rate of progress of women and minorities in leadership roles. We need to look at how much our workforce changes, year after year, within all bands.

Source: "The Company Defines Diversity as a Competitive Advantage", AlliedSignal Engineered Materials Employee Newsletter *Matters*, November 1994.

**Note**

Make no mistake: The pressure on you to continuously improve will soon ease as China begins enforcing its laws on intellectual property[23]. So if you develop successful operations before the coming wave of legal enforcement, you will establish a sound model that "advantages" your business both domestically and globally.

To accelerate your preparation for China-based success, we offer one of the top MBA schools' case study approach to illustrate business situations in China. With five case studies (see Section V), you will develop a range of new thinking for handling different risks and business conflicts–all part and parcel of many operations.

We ask you, first, to complete the worksheets we offer along the way, beginning with the *Chapter 1* Worksheet (see next page). This prepares you for your "30 Minute Workbook" in *Chapter 10*–which tackles several areas sure to have a big impact on you. (We welcome further thoughts and comments on all the issues discussed here. Contact information for making recommendations is available at the end of the book.)

*It is better to light a candle than to complain about the darkness.*

—R. Herzog

# CHAPTER 1
# WORKSHEET

1. My market potential in China is: _____ in _____ industry(ies) I am now in Phase (check one): ___Four ___Five ___Six of the Business Life Cycle.

2. We project sales of _____ within _____ years and my reasonable profit as a percent of sales is _____%.

This is based on:
___External Consultants ___ Internal Teams ___Other_____

3. The following are my 3 key assumptions in the China market:

[Example: One standard assumption covers the economic conditions you presume to be operating in China.]

| Assumption | Date of last update | Source |
|---|---|---|
| a. _____ | _____ | _____ |
| b. _____ | _____ | _____ |
| c. _____ | _____ | _____ |

4. My investment in equipment and facilities is US$_____ which can be used over _____ years. My reasonable return as a percent of this investment is _____%.

At the moment-___ I am close to ___ I am not close to achieving that return today, but may in ___ years.

I have ____ ventures operating now, all averaging _____annual sales

My Key Issues in China:

_____

_____

_____

*Know thyself and thy enemy,*
*and you shall be undefeated.*

*—Sun Tsu, The Art of War*

# Chapter 2

# Understand your goals in China

<u>Note</u>

## *Executive Summary*

- *KEY: **What is your goal in China?** Remember: Skills for lining up suppliers are different from those used to attract customers.*

- *Your critical **success path requires tools** to prioritize your resources and differentiate your business. These tools must also help you communicate and tackle continuous improvement.*

- *For **some helpful examples**, we'll glance at snapshots of Coca Cola, Pepsi, Honeywell, R. R. Donnelley, and McDonald's.*

**Do you have what it takes to operate in China?**

Even if you're competing and winning at home, your product or service may not be ready for the China market. For one thing, your Core Competence[20] may not be truly global. Consider this problem from the context of a local newspaper. The <u>Sun Gazette</u> newspaper–serving a suburban area of northern Virginia (McLean, Vienna, Oakton)–is popular among Washington, DC area readers. But it surely lacks the right content for a global audience. <u>USA Today</u>, on the other hand, was first greeted with lots of skepticism, all suggesting a national newspaper would offer only superficial coverage of issues. Yet today, a growing numbers of "road warriors" have made <u>USA Today</u> the highest circulation paper, and it is now available in most major hotels worldwide.

Only some products can be "globally appropriate."

But you're not alone in wanting to "go global." You may have followed your customers to this global market. Or maybe you've identified suitable suppliers already there. We see products imported into the US everyday. For example, Hewlett Packard ink cartridges are made elsewhere (not in the US), and Haier refrigerators sold at the Yale campus book store are, in fact, produced by a Chinese owned company based here.

You know some of the issues behind international business start-ups in China. Rest assured: We'll offer you a much deeper perspective in subsequent pages. One thing is certain: Without knowing the culture, buying habits and business demands in any one country, you will fail even if you uncover attractive opportunities. That's especially true in China.

**First Questions**

What separates the winners from the losers in new China businesses? You may have heard about the value of "Guanxi" or relationships. The value of that idea, and its application, has been somewhat exaggerated

"Guanxi," plain and simple, is the knack of managing your Chinese relationships. But remember: Before you need "Guanxi," you need much more. For starters, focus on and clarify your overall goals. Clarify that, and you have clearer "sailing" in the China market. Then you can turn to "Guanxi" to shape your implementation of your business plans.

Are you looking for customers, or suppliers to export out of China? If you want customers, will you import into China, or set up an entity in China? If you plan to establish an entity, what are the key attributes you seek? Operational control? Majority ownership, if not wholly owned?

While these questions may seem rhetorical since many companies already have a presence in China, your priorities will change as your executive teams evolve at your home office or in China. Let's focus harder on what you want to do first.

Let's say you have a variety of products or services, and want to do what it takes to turn a profit. Here, you must pinpoint your capabilities, and you then can rely on Guanxi to define the right execution strategy. Remember, though: Without core competencies, you may have short term gains, but this is "fool's gold" and will soon fail.

If you want low cost suppliers, you need 3 elements to successfully establish low-cost supplier relationships:

- **Documentation**

  Document your products or services and make this available in detail so that suppliers understand the product. If the drawings for products are out of date, or if standard work practices (e.g., how phones should be answered in a call center) are unclear, you will be plagued with confusion and miscommunication.

- **Sourcing Selection Criteria**

  Create selection criteria for suppliers so you can benefit from objective decision making processes. Often, there is no "ideal" supplier. So, given your data on all suppliers' strengths and weaknesses, you will have to decide what you can live with.

- **A quality focused supply strategy**

  You need a supply strategy based on continuous improvement just to develop an efficient supply chain. You will also need to neutralize your weakest point in that chain[24] to sustain profitable growth. Remember: Your weakest link in the chain will change as you improve your supply procedures–so constantly review your processes, and your chain's "links."

Similarly, you need other strategic steps to impact the China market with your products or services:

- **Identify your product's value in China**

  Do you know what your Chinese customers say about your product—how they value it? First, use assumptions to set up your initial efforts; then validate your assumptions after entry.

- **Establish clear market entry definitions**

  Develop a market entry strategy establishing the right geography, the right product or service, and the team responsible for execution. Since China is bigger than the US (in size and population), be sure to pick your entry point carefully.

- **Develop a quality-focused customer service strategy**

  Not only must you know your customers' views of your product, you must understand customer preferences and "deliver" these preferences cost effectively. Obviously, if you target customer service, you improve customers' satisfaction and create business.

Remember, too, that you have two teams to nurture: First, the team responsible for finding low cost suppliers; also, the team responsible for market-entry into the China market.

Both require very different skills, and it's your job to ensure they have these skills.

Start by focusing on your target customers and you will know how to handle the two teams. If you already have a well-tested continuous improvement process in your domestic Business Life Cycle (Phases 1-3), you have tools for communicating expectations across both teams—thereby creating a more optimal China startup timeline.

To understand how thorough this process can be, let's consider a "real time" example: Danaher (Danaher Business System, or DBS), a successful manufacturer and quality process leader (See Exhibit 2-1). DBS's process starts with the Voice Of the Customer (VOC), which is screened through Quality, Delivery, and Cost (QDC) dimensions to provide DBS's customer satisfaction. The foundation of this success is world class quality prioritized by Policy Deployment matrices, which in turn drive

**Exhibit 2-1**
**Danaher Business System**

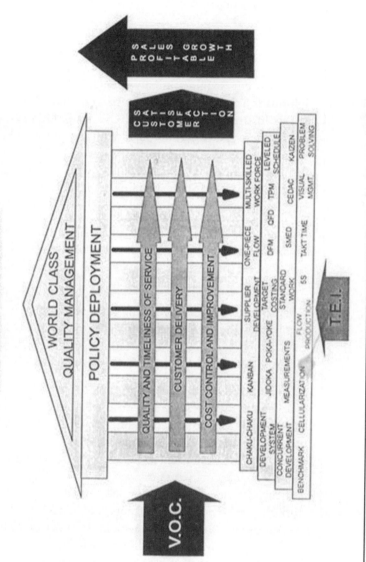

Source: Raymond James & Associates, Inc. Special Situations Report on Danaher Corporation, St. Petersburg, Florida, 1995

high QDC–all this is possible by leveraging tools and methods available to DBS employees through Total Employee Involvement (TEI).

The DBS process is complex, but it is necessary. Danaher's former CEO George Sherman long ago realized one thing about the company's China operation. DBS's market entry had great potential but required highly-detailed, and reliable market information to execute growth in Asia, especially Greater China. For its Instrument and Control (IC) Group, DBS evaluated its Asian market potential thoroughly. In that process, then-CEO Sherman courted other global companies, e.g., Fluke, an instrumentation and test product producer with a known brand in China. Eventually, Sherman purchased Fluke to make DBS's core IC business.

One measure of success in this process: Danaher now enjoys premium stock valuation via high price/earnings ratios, and positive support from Wall Street investment analysts' evaluations.

To reiterate: Selling to 1.3 billion potential customers is an idea that may concentrate your mind, but it may not work. China is vast, with many more ethnic minorities than in the US. Despite tremendous strides in communications during the 20th century, it is still difficult to sell to ALL Chinese. Images of foreigners remain less-than-positive.

The mosaic that is China is indeed extensive. Many in northeastern China harbor vivid, painful memories of World War II and Japanese atrocities there, including evidence of biological experimentation on Chinese citizens. On the western side, the native language citizens in western cities like Urumqi in Xinjiang Province is the language of Islamic peoples (Arabic, Turkish, and Persian/Farsi), not of Chinese. A Cantonese speaker can not communicate with his fellow citizen who speaks only Mandarin. Meanwhile, though Mandarin is used throughout Greater China, most Hong Kong residents can not communicate fluently in Mandarin.

Geographically, China's most developed region lies along the coast, from Hong Kong and Hainan (south), through Taiwan and Fujian (east), to Qingdao, Tianjin, and port cities like Dalian in the north.

[**NOTE:** Since we're not targeting all Greater China markets, we'll defer discussion of Taiwan and Hong Kong until *Chapter 8.*]

## Geographic and other decision points

If you plan to sell consumer products, you will set up "shop" in China's coastal regions. But if you want to sell industrial products, you should plan to sell throughout China–after you establish your target customers.

Some help is on hand. If you want suppliers and you have well documented products or services, the Chinese have well developed trading logistics to help you, especially when there is technology transfer and the products are exported out of China. Your suppliers often receive special incentives (tax rebates) and access to foreign currency to export their products.

Given the still partially-enforced intellectual property laws, the burden of protecting your products falls on your team charged with finding suppliers. In this process, it's vital to avoid mistakes: Paying too much, not knowing hidden costs, or relying excessively on middlemen.

*How do you protect yourself against mistakes?* Don't accept what appears to be an attractive price. Quiz people about their assumptions, ask questions from new perspectives, and above all, compare. Obviously, these are business basics, but you must come armed with many tactics. Discussions are tricky given the timing of payment, the interpretation of contract terms, management of logistics, and your "degrees of freedom" in negotiations. In such cases, miscommunications are common, and to cite a saying common in business, "assume" can mean making an "ass" out of "u" and "me." (Needless to add, lawyers have thriving law practices that handle these difficulties and other problems with assumptions.)

In short, the road to China profits is paved with obstacles. To ride that road, you need a clear understanding of both customers and competitors, and you'll need teams armed with flexible tools and processes to meet your particular customer needs.

The following 4 mini-cases highlight the basis for some foreign companies' operations in China. [**NOTE**: We sidestep Chinese negotiation style here because there are excellent books on the topic[25, 26].]

### 4 Mini-Cases: Coca Cola, Pepsi, Honeywell, R.R. Donnelley

Consider, for starters, the lessons learned by Coca Cola. <u>Fortune</u> magazine has called "Coke" the "best" brand in the world. Its tremendous brand equity is driven by many features, and these include serious market testing and careful planning. Armed with its "secret syrup" formula (known to a precious few), Coca Cola's challenges in China are to package the product with strong, thorough marketing strategy. The company's three main products, Coca Cola, Sprite, and Fanta, have well-defined consumer target groups, and its ad campaigns zero in on the fashionable, trendy and young. The key to success is to deliver value to the consumers by

- Economies of scale that allow an affordable price
- Availability to all consumers through a strong distribution system

In China, the company worked with strong partners, Swire, Kerry, and Cofco, and it leveraged its partners' local experience and focused on building a strong distribution system as soon as China opened her doors in 1978. 21 plants went up quickly; at least 30 were operating in 2003.

By contrast, Pepsi's strategy focused on company-funded investments, starting with fewer bottling plants (about a dozen) and without the benefit of local experience. Pepsi may not be as successful yet, but they invested heavily in the "Blue" campaign in the late 1990s and have started to penetrate the China market. Pepsi used 100% local Chinese singers for its campaign, and focused on a "fresh and young" feeling in its ads. By sustaining this momentum towards the Beijing 2008 Olympics, Pepsi should also be successful in this market.

Another success story is AlliedSignal (now Honeywell). It began investing in China long before ex-Chairman and CEO Larry

Bossidy acquired Honeywell. For five years beginning in 1996, AlliedSignal's most profitable investment in China was the maintenance, repair, and overhaul of a very profitable aerospace division called Aircraft Landing Systems (ALS). At the heart of this business was the brake pad business, especially the older steel brakes and newer carbon brakes. After spending millions of dollars to receive US Federal Aviation Administration (FAA) approval and the support of aircraft manufacturers like Boeing, these products are priced to recapture the original investment and its risks. To remain current, AlliedSignal developed a series of documentation binders in different languages for each model of aircraft. These are updated regularly to ensure continued compliance with the latest rules on airworthiness.

Going into the process, Honeywell knew it would have nightmares if its products could not be sold to airline customers after all the initial investment. Precisely this nightmare materialized when the Chinese developed their own brake pad products certified by the Chinese government. To parry this development, Honeywell created a win-win strategic solution through a joint venture (JV) with a customer (China Eastern Airlines). The JV was charged with maintaining, repairing, and overhauling all wheels and brakes in China for all airlines. In 2003, this JV is still a leader in China and the only Chinese business certified by both (the US) FAA and the Chinese Civil Aviation Administration of China (CAAC) exclusively for wheels and brakes. It has established a niche and must continue to improve by adding services and competitive prices. Otherwise it will be difficult to extend this JV's life, as competitors are lurking for their chance in the market.

One more example: R. R. Donnelley. This was the first major foreign investor in China's printing industry. It has a super majority ownership of a printing facility in southern China that, under the WTO schedule, can not be duplicated until some time after 2005. The China market is so attractive that a heavy investment on a second facility is starting up in Shanghai, this time with initial minority ownership. As in many industrial facilities, the price and variable margin of printing must be sufficiently high to recapture the fixed asset investments in web presses and the facility. Since printing is a restricted industry in China, R. R. Donnelley's approved business and printing licenses are valuable. To continuously improve and successfully compete, it must train and develop the workforce for superior print quality, and significantly enhance services. Otherwise competitors will begin to impact its profitability.

Finally, a word about McDonald's which, like Kentucky Fried Chicken, began building Chinese brand equity in the early 1990s[27]. McDonald's advertised and built many new facilities by the late 1990s. A well publicized incident related to its franchise near Beijing's Tiananmen Square where the strict enforcement of Chinese land use rights laws drove its demolition. This case sparked many activities, complicated by alleged government corruption. It highlighted the need to better understand the legal environment as the Chinese government attempts to avoid inconsistent enforcement of laws and regulations.

Now it's your turn. Use the Worksheet to help you define and communicate your goals in China so your teammates know what needs to be accomplished.

*Be who you are and say what you feel, because those who mind don't matter and those who matter don't mind.*

*—Dr. Seuss*

# CHAPTER 2
# WORKSHEET

1. My target in China is to find:
   a. Local suppliers _____
   b. Trading partners _____
   c. Joint venture partners _____
   d. Technologies _____
   e. Local employees _____
   f. Consultants _____
   g. Customers _____

2. The features of the process I have: _____
   This is strong in _____
   And weak in _____

3. My process that I plan to use focuses on:
   a. Financial information _____
   b. Customer information _____
   c. Market/competitor information _____
   d. Production quality _____
   e. Resource allocation _____
   f. Distribution _____

4. Companies most appealing to me in China are: _____

   _____

5.  The information most useful to me in China includes: _____

_____

Key issues I see in my products' or services' features and benefits:

Features: _____

_____

Benefits: _____

_____

*Do not confuse motion and progress.*
*A rocking horse keeps moving but does not make any progress.*

*—Alfred A. Montapert*

# Section II

# Managing success means achieving your goals through your expatriates

By now, you know your goals in China and you're ready to create your "operations arm." No matter how much money or equipment you have, the truth is that you cannot manage success yourself. You must execute through people.

As the Nike commercial says, "No one can do it alone."

Who <u>will</u> help you execute? Your team–"road warriors" and expatriates–knows your goals and how you want to execute. By definition, your road warriors aren't the people "on the ground" so they cannot comprise the team that effectively delivers growth.

That role, the role of change agents, is up to your expatriates. In short, they carry your core competencies to China. Once there, they train local Chinese managers to sustain your growth.

In reality, of course, your "expats" live in China, and leave their home office jobs to do this. But when they leave, you backfill those expatriates' home office jobs.

**What's wrong with this picture?** With no clear repatriation plans, your expatriates have nothing to return to–after success in China. This is what keeps many from taking on overseas postings in general, and from going to China in particular.

37

**To address this imbalance and lack of job security, we'll help you find new ways to motivate expatriates.**

"Motivate," says the Merriam-Webster dictionary, means you "provide…a need" that drives further action. To motivate your team in China to deliver results, you must create a "need" (the expat assignment), and let them "act" (deliver profitable sales).

**Your available tools** for creating a need include

- Incentive compensation.
- Family benefits, including family housing and education for the expatriates' children.
- Career satisfaction and long term career growth.

**For any assignment in China, you simply must factor in the impact on an expatriate's family. As in our earlier discussion of the Business Life Cycle, let's set up a framework for discussing expatriate careers.**

**If we're examining individual careers and their links to families, the Career Life Cycle's 4 Segments (Exhibit II-1) look something like this:**

1   **First 5 years' experience**–few if any family obligations

2   **5-20 years experience**–growing families in primary schools

3   **20-30 years experience**–with children in high schools or universities

4   **30+years experience**–with grown adult children

**Two other moments are equally relevant in such discussions:**

- When the first child is born. The lifestyle changes drastically and medical care becomes very important. This generally correlates to employees in segment 2 with 5-20 years work experience.
- As children begin to attend college and become independent adults. This generally correlates with employees in Segment 3 (20-30 years' experience).

When applying this framework in "real time" (and individual situations may call for varying approaches), we see that Segment

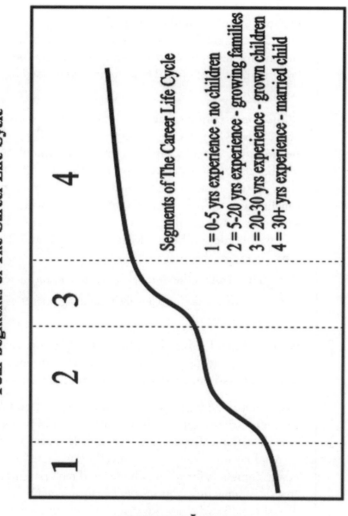

Exhibit II-1

Four Segments of The Career Life Cycle

Segments of The Career Life Cycle

1 = 0-5 yrs experience - no children
2 = 5-20 yrs experience - growing families
3 = 20-30 yrs experience - grown children
4 = 30+ yrs experience - married child

1  2  3  4

Job Responsibilities

Experience

1 employees may lack the experience to clearly articulate and drive any new business. Segment 4 people, meanwhile, may prefer maintaining their status quo (given their 30 years' experience), and might opt out of leading new business initiatives in China.

**In short, your top candidates are those in Segments 2 and 3 of their career cycles.** Most of these will have school-aged children and attend religious (usually) church services, most likely as Protestants or Catholics. These are important demographics to keep in mind.

**While most families have children, many expatriates have none. Why? Cost is a big driver in selection.** For each expatriate child, the cost of a typical international school "allowance" will be US$20,000 per year, or US$30,000-35,000 after tax gross up (if Chinese taxes are included). With such high child benefit costs, employers may prefer families without children when screening candidates for overseas assignments. This action may well border on being illegal (in the US), and it can harm expats over time because

- This reduces the number of qualified candidates, and
- Employees do not view overseas assignments as critical to their careers.

**We recommend some "breakthrough" thinking.** Avoid focusing on cost, and target instead the benefits in your messages: **Insist that "assignments in China are good for careers."**

**Then, as you address expatriate family issues (see *Chapter 5*), your expatriates can focus far more on driving profitable growth-without distractions.** Remember: A key goal for you is to avoid creating long term ("career") expatriates; instead, find new assignments for them at home, and repatriate your expatriates. By doing this, you create a team of managers strong in diversity skills who are loyal and productive over the "long haul." Repeat this several times, and you'll see employees competing for China assignments. You can then pick the best strategy to expanding China operations and achieving even higher profits-because you'll have the "horses" for that race.

**You can thereby create a cycle that feeds on itself: Superior employees delivering growth and better managers, and more growth. This is clearly a win-win solution.**

As we continue to pinpoint new ways to achieve your goals through expatriates, we will tap the experiences of Mark Chen in our case studies to illustrate key issues along the way. A Case Study #3 Summary is presented on the next two pages for your reference.

## KEY READER REFERENCE

### CASE STUDY #3 – CASE SUMMARY
### "ASH Conglomerate's Operations in China"

*(Note:   Section V contains five case studies   written in the style taught at top MBA schools around the world.   This summary is for your reference only.)*

### Executive Summary

At ASH Conglomerate, a US$25 billion North American industrial corporation, its Aerospace Equipment Systems (AES) unit had US$2 billion in global sales when Mark Chen assumed the role of (Asia) Director of Business Development.

Teamed with sales and supported by the US home office, Mark Chen negotiated and managed ASH's first profitable Chinese JV. This case study shows how a trained cadre of local Chinese employees can gear up to deliver high productivity (higher even than a similar US workforce) within 6 months of start up – and capture the full value of low cost (but well-trained) labor.

### Background

ASH Conglomerate began a self-assessment of growth opportunities and combined this with its traditional encouragement for top managers to help grow the company. A veteran Asian American employee, Mark was familiar with the company culture when he took on the role of developing Asian business for AES.

**Key Points:**   1) Mark knew the features of ASH's healthy growth culture.
2) ASH established and committed itself to growth in Asia.

Convinced this was part of a successful career growth path, Mark diligently pursued attractive growth opportunities throughout Asia. He negotiated royalties for technology transfers to Japan, and prioritized opportunities and resources as he worked with sales teams to support additional growth in business.

As Mark met Chinese customers, he saw opportunities for ASH to become an industry leader in China in servicing aircraft.   The Chinese customers were:

1) Paying a high price to service many assemblies overseas, and
2) Incurring significant packaging and shipping expenses for transportation

Mark pursued these opportunities by proposing win-win solutions: Selling ASH products and servicing both ASH and competitor products within China.  As Chinese customers began to see how his proposals could expand their service business to the entire industry, Mark's ASH Sales team was awarded new sales contracts, and Mark, in turn, negotiated a profitable services JV.

## Execution

For 15 months, Mark averaged 80 hours of monthly air travel during the negotiations and start-up phases of the JV. Geographically, the strategy was prepared in Indiana, reviewed in Tokyo and Hong Kong, negotiated in Shanghai, and approved in California and New Jersey. On the Chinese side, the business license was issued in Shanghai. CAAC certification was approved in Beijing, and US FAA certification was approved in Singapore. In short, it was a complex process, but handled deftly.

**Key Points**: 1) Mark was a self motivated expatriate focused on results.
2) Work-Life balance issues for him were minimal.

After Mark secured the JV's business license, he pursued a concurrent strategy for recruiting and training the workforce (in the US) while other teams worked on purchasing equipment, building the facility, and translating and documenting the key operating procedures into Chinese.

Once the workforce completed its training in the US, the team moved to its new facility in China. By then, equipment had already been installed and the operating procedures already translated into Chinese.

The new JV facility and its entirely local Chinese workforce passed FAA and CAAC certifications on the first attempt, and achieved ISO9002 and High Technology Enterprise designations quickly – two difficult certification milestones.

With the internal control procedures customized from the US operation, initial products were accepted by the customers without exception.

## Outcome

When its workforce productivity was benchmarked, the JV offered comparable or faster turnaround time than similar US units – within six months of startup. By eliminating transport costs, AES's customers saved money. And with its lower-cost labor pool, the JV's profitability was higher than the US operation.

The JV's success attracted attention. It was featured on the cover of the (conglomerate's) 1995 Annual Report.

**Key Points:**  1) The local Chinese in this China-based operation learned to execute quickly once they were trained in the know-how required.
2) Core competencies needed:
- Certifications from FAA and CAAC
- Motivated local Chinese workforce
- Quality and Inventory Control of Airworthy parts and assemblies
- Superior service and competitive pricing

To sustain this profitable JV operation, the Six Sigma quality training process was implemented. As a result, this JV remains a stellar performer today.

\*\*\*

*The power of accurate observation is
frequently called cynicism by those who don't have it.*

*—George Bernard Shaw (1856-1950)*

# Chapter 3

# Recruit and develop your expatriates

Note

### *Executive Summary*

- *With an 8-step framework, we help you identify **2 key selection criteria** for recruiting expatriates:*
  - *They need to be culturally sensitive, and*
  - *They must be strong coaches.*
- *As you **share your market research information** internally, you build strong employee communities interested in overseas businesses.*
- *Beware this management issue: Your overseas assignments may not be "success tracks" to progressively successful careers–which critically impacts the value of your US$30-50 billion annual investment. Solution: Upgrade your handling of "expats"–ensure you successfully repatriate them since they are your "first team offense" for managing a diverse and inclusive workforce.*

**How do you know you are ready to go overseas?** What are the internal and external signals?

There is no single, definitive answer for most companies. Depending on your company size, you usually *think* you're

44

ready when your sales staff gets an overseas inquiry, and through further negotiations, you get a Purchase Order.

The scenario beyond this is fairly predictable. More POs pour in, and you sales people launch their overseas travel. On that foreign turf, you set up customer meetings, product training, trade shows–and, more travel. This is a typical passive start to launch your overseas business.

Is "passive" strategy adequate for future demands? Hardly.

### Passive versus Assertive Strategy

If instead you shift to an assertive posture, you can begin today to initiate self-assessments of your China opportunities. Premier companies typically have internal processes to push such initiatives. If you sponsor this initiative, you may well find employees like our case study manager Mark Chen (ASH Conglomerate–*Case #3*) who will help you drive your initiative to fruition in Asia.

### Early Investor Status

In China, you get more flexibility and control whenever you stake a claim as an early investor. In two of our case studies, ABC Printing (*Case #5*) and ASH Conglomerate (*Case #3*), you'll find majority owned Joint Ventures (JVs) that cannot be replicated even by aggressive competitors until 2006. These majority ownership entities automatically have several years' head-start–creating formidable market-entry barriers–in their markets of choice.

But there are more issues: Unless you are ready, your early investment may be a liability, as ABC Printing (*Case #5*) demonstrates. Majority ownership does not mean *profit*. Without a leader "on the ground" or an appropriate culture, you will lose money even in China.

Your first line of defense against all of these initial issues: **Prepare the ground for your operations with a careful staff selection strategy.**

Let's go through selected stages of a self-assessment that will help you identify and develop your key expatriates. For the moment, we're focusing only on expatriates. You will see a more complete discussion for delivering profitable growth in *Chapters 6, 7, and 8*. And in *Chapter 9*, you will see a recap of all these vital steps—before you complete your first self-assessment in *Chapter 10's "30 Minute Workbook."*

**Staff Selection and Management Framework**

The following 8 steps focus on the pivotal role of your expatriates in your China-based operation, and how you can support them. The process ends with their repatriation—which is a transition point to further success in China using local Chinese talent.

### Key Selection and Management Steps

1. Do market research to understand your specific market drivers.

2. Allocate resources to confirm that you have the key features of an attractive market.

3. Establish your main market expectations for your company.

4. For your key step, **select culturally sensitive employees** who can value overseas assignments, and who can serve as **helpful coaches** "on the ground" in China.

5. Customize individual expectations by alerting your line managers, and support this with forceful Human Resource policies.

6. Maintain continuity of home office support and raise the visibility of new career opportunities for expats on overseas assignments.

7. Prime the ground for overseas "tours" with a strong succession plan for China, preferably by developing and coaching local talent.

8. When appropriate, repatriate your China-based expats, and show how their overseas experience is part of a successful career path in your home office. Champion these career paths as steps that are vital to your company's growth domestically and globally.

China, remember, remains an emerging market. On average, a non-Chinese funded enterprise has US$12 million sales annually. And, **few foreign companies are "big" in China.** Fewer than 10 foreign companies exceed US$2 billion in annual sales there, and these include Motorola, Volkswagen and some other global multinationals.

But with China's entry into the WTO (2001), there's good news: China now offers an accelerated growth phase for foreign businesses aiming to scale up.

To participate in this accelerated growth, prepare the ground carefully, so you can benefit quickly. You need an effective, diverse workforce and, for good measure, well-documented scalable processes.

**Your first questions: Who are your strong candidates** with 5-30 years' experience ready to drive the growth of an overseas business? **What are their profiles** and **how can these overseas assignments help your company**, and simultaneously enhance their career prospects? These are important questions before you seek and recruit the best candidates.

Most employers are much stronger in establishing market expectations than in successfully repatriating your staffers. Many believe people are among their most valuable assets.

But are these the assumptions that drive your own planning for China operations? To unbundle some of the issues for expatriates here, let's look at each step of this process more closely.

*Step 1: Do market research to assess your specific market drivers.*

You can use many approaches to find the right market or partners in China. Most likely, your initial efforts included external consultants or business development/marketing employees from the home office, supported by the sales staffers responsible for China sales.

Who plays which role? Business people say that *marketing* needs to "have the right products to offer," while *sales* has the job of "moving the products." Your business development team has to assess the key priorities for your product mix. If you haven't done this already, ensure that your development teams' experiences are documented in your company's memory–either as a Business Development or Market Research Libraries, or as a "knowledge management system."

**Example**: If you archive your past presentations and studies, you shorten the cycle time for new development steps, and help strengthen the community of internal candidates who want overseas assignments. In smaller businesses, a simple file folder (or bookshelf) may work well.

> In our Genteli Telecom case (*Case #4*), we show how a market must be prioritized according to available resources. By trying to serve both the retail and wholesale markets, Genteli was not able to deliver basic customer services. But once it focused on wholesale customers, Genteli quickly met its startup milestones and did not have to forfeit all of its US$6.4 million Performance Bond.

*Step 2: Allocate resources to confirm you have the key features of an attractive market.*

As long as you believe China is an attractive market, you can use your teamwork to help prioritize your market opportunities.

To accelerate progress, you may consider a concurrent analysis and execution strategy. For example, instead of just conducting product seminars to explore prospective customer reaction, add a sales staffer to your seminar to help sell your products–and to subsidize your market research cost and gain experience going through the steps of selling in China. Some examples from our case studies will illustrate this.

> In our D Conglomerate case (*Case #2*), a US based Marketing team worked closely with its China based business development team to prioritize industry characteristics. The focus was on power quality and reliability, and other specialty niche markets. In this continuous process through Policy Deployment, D Conglomerate successfully assessed the readiness of its home office for creating a team and pursuing its overseas opportunities.

- The market research cost was partially financed by export sales into China
- The flexibility offered by a Policy Deployment process allowed periodic updates and reduced the number of assumptions before making any investment decisions
- The team decision also affirmed home office support.

Meanwhile, in the ASH Conglomerate case (*Case #3*), Mark Chen leveraged the JV investment as a competitive advantage to the customer purchase decision. He focused on customer requirements and openly communicated these to the JV team. The Chinese skills were then in full view, once the JV delivered profit within 6 months of the business license. All this required that the

- local Chinese workforce was recruited in China
- workforce was trained and certified in the US
- facility was built
- equipment was purchased, imported and installed
- operating procedures were translated and documented
- US and Chinese governments certified that the JV delivers airworthy parts
- customers accepted the initial products without exception.

In Genteli Telecom (*Case #4*), a cross functional team of sales, marketing and engineering sprang into action to reorganize and sell successfully to wholesale customers.

Finally, in the T Conglomerate case (*Case #1*), several examples:

- ADZ operations was set up in Taiwan with teammates from Singapore.
- Fire extinguisher manufacturing was successfully transferred from Japan to China. The transfer price was established only after the Japanese Quality

Manager and Engineering Manager validated the quality of the Chinese product. The win-win solution was established when Japan operation paid a lower price for the product, and the Chinese operation benefited over time with component localization cost savings.

*Step 3: Establish the main market expectations for your company.*

If you rely on business projections to set incentive plan targets, you will see a full discussion of this in *Chapter 4*. But you should embrace many assessments related to resources, customer acceptance, quality and product performance to help drive your market expectations.

Most of you establish annual market expectations keyed to a long term strategic plan. Periodically (quarterly basis for industrial products, daily or weekly for fast moving consumer products), you will use financial forecasts to drive management resource allocation decisions.

**Consider one "tweak" to this approach:** You can gain flexibility thru Danaher's policy deployment tactics that link resources to market expectations. The strength of Danaher's Policy Deployment includes:

- An interconnected set of documents that allocate resources according to broadly-established priorities.

- Exception-based management where only deviations require top management to intervene in decisions. Most often this is driven by new information related to assumptions in Policy Deployment.

- DBS has the flexibility to adjust these targets as new information becomes available. The adjustments usually change available resources to strengthen the team capabilities.

In short, if you link your long range strategic plan, annual budget, and your forecast to resource allocations, you will succeed. The more flexible your process, the faster your pace of adjustments to changing market conditions.

At the very foundation of these assumptions, of course, is the idea that there is integrity in your systems. If your process lacks reliable information to start, you will face confusion and counter-productive efforts. In this case, you'll face the old cliché: Garbage in, garbage out.

*Step 4: For your key step, select culturally sensitive employees who can value overseas assignments, and who can serve as coaches "on the ground" in China.*

You probably have a process to identify interested expatriate candidates. To ensure a greater probability of success, initiate training and ensure that it is fully implemented. Counter-example: Though ABC Printing (in *Case #5*) had such a process in place, it was not fully implemented. As a result, that company's Mark Chen completed his 2-year program in 8 months.

Remember, too, to develop your Business Development or Market Research Library. Gather together abbreviated presentations that can be discussed with interested employees. Then use this knowledge to promote your company's long range plans and give your employees a chance to contribute to overseas growth.

Motivating employee communities to see win-win interests in overseas assignments is not difficult. You must facilitate a forum for communicating with your employees, and show them they will be rewarded at the completion of their overseas tour.

> In companies like AT&T, managers sponsor regular events like Lunar Spring Festival dinners, and Mid-Autumn Festival celebrations to spur the creation of employee communities interested in Chinese business. (Where appropriate, these activities can be extended to other ethnic celebrations such as Kwaanza and Hanukkah.) All this promotion significantly enhances the development a global company culture.

> Employees will be very interested, especially if senior managers champion these events, appear at them, and commit time to fully support these activities. You can convert what might seem purely social gatherings by adding speakers and even brief presentations that educate as well as entertain.

You should openly discuss company positions on various China issues once you create this employee forum. "Put" these communities online to encourage discussions about business and career opportunities. (You can moderate these chats by representatives of the Human Resources department.) Rest assured: You will find interested employee candidates.

Your employees, after all, have diverse interests. Caucasian employees will have an interest in Chinese culture; Chinese-Americans will be interested in their heritage. (Some may not be interested in career or business aspects, so be prepared to see some who don't share your goals.)

**The key success factor is consistent top management commitment** visibly reinforced in company communications. Highlight your competitive advantages and empower employees to carry your message forward to their own communities. Provide continuity for overseas employees and a forum to re-connect with your home office via online communities. As your online communities mature, encourage overseas employees to extend an active online community to local employees outside the US. The cost of this investment will pay for itself by reduced printing costs for newsletters, by lower turnover, and by higher sales.

For employees interested in overseas assignments, you pique their curiosity because they

- Enjoy traveling and/or the foreign culture
- Want to live overseas for a few years
- Wish to live overseas and stay overseas
- Want to contribute to overseas growth
- See their own skill sets can be developed
- View overseas assignments as a true career growth path
- Plan to retire overseas

While these are personal reasons for taking on overseas tours, the company rationale is not far behind. Employees you recruit will be both loyal and productive if you understand their many motivations for taking on overseas tours of duty.

Since your top candidates for overseas assignments are usually excellent employees, your big question remains: **"How do we avoid disrupting successful domestic career paths with overseas assignments?**

**The answer: Ensure career continuity**, motivate employees to deliver results and return them to your home office. In other words, all China assignments should be part of a career growth path.

Moreover, you should strongly encourage overseas-bound staffers to develop a pool of local talent as quickly as possible. Your goal with overseas assignments, remember, is not to deliver fish to China, but to teach local employees how to fish. The difference: Deliver fish, and your Chinese employees rely on expatriates to operate. Teach local employees to fish, and they will grow and thrive on their own. Where appropriate, your repatriated employees can continue to supervise local Chinese employees from your home office.

To recap: Two key selection criteria are critical.

- **Find employees interested in China business and culture.**

  You need employees who are culturally sensitive. It is less important for them to speak Chinese than to be technical experts and culturally sensitive ones. For an excellent summary of what "culturally sensitive" means, see Scott Seligman's *"Chinese Business Etiquette"*[28]. In addition, psychological inventories like WJ Reddin's "Culture Shock Inventory" (distributed by Wu & Associates LLC[29]) may also help.

- **Find employees who can be strong coaches for developing local talent.**

  Given two giant costs–your cost of not retaining local talent, and the big outlays for assigning your expatriates overseas–your potential expenses are enormous. So it will repay your efforts handsomely if you can avoid incurring additional costs in China.

  Language is not a prerequisite to cultural sensitivity, but you enhance the credibility of your expats if they're trained to use the language. Said differently: Lack of language skills in coaches will raise your cost of China-based operations. Few local employees are bi-lingual, and because of their scarcity, they command substantial premiums in compensation. And many more competent employees in China cannot communicate fluently in English. The more fluent English speakers usually are ex-English majors, limited in handling business or engineering issues.

To illustrate from our case studies, Mark Chen grew ABC Printing in China (*Case #5*) via Pre-Media core competencies and providing quality training in Chinese-and there were other successes (see *Cases #3* and *#1*). After Mark's tenure in his assignment, however, the imperative for finding culturally sensitive expatriates took priority over developing strong coaches, as all three companies found Caucasian males with no language abilities. Result: Since these expats were not strong coaches, their prospects of becoming "career" expatriates increased dramatically.

*Step 5: Customize individual expectations by alerting your line managers, and support this with forceful HR policies.*

While market expectations drive performance targets, individual expatriates need clearly delineated Letters of Understanding (LOU) that reflect an agreement between them and their supervisors. The focus: The LOU should detail what the China assignment is expected to accomplish. Equally important: The length of the overseas tour of duty, and the expectations for the expatriate at the end of his assignment.

How do you start this customizing process? Use the 2 selection criteria already cited: Cultural sensitivity and commitment to develop local talent. Tell the expatriates you plan to use tools such as "360 degree surveys" to get performance input from their superiors, peers, and subordinates. Another set of tools: An assessment that gives you the number of local managers and their responsibilities-in short, the speed of localization. These are measurable tools to gauge the progress of your expatriates.

Recognize, also, that there are 2 types of expatriates:

- *Those who want to perform and return to the home office*

  With these, maintaining continuity with the home office is critical. After all, they expect to be back at the home office.

- *Those who want to perform and stay overseas*

  Additional overseas assignments are important for these, so their "Personal Development Plans" should be focused on this.

To create win-win solutions for both types, demonstrate your company's commitment to

- Finding future opportunities for expatriate managers.

- Giving these expats new responsibilities as local managers offload their (expatriates') workload.

- Sharing your business plan so your expats understand how they can justify long term expatriate assignments.

And there may be personal issues that should be understood by your line or functional managers before expatriates are sent to China. HR staffers are facilitators, and they can help you in communicating to line managers.

Let's stress the core company culture issue: Open communications and multiple channels of communication. You should communicate what's known and what's not, because expectations must be flexible enough to change with constantly "churning" information. This is the foundation for continuous improvement, and why Danaher's DBS has been successful. To paraphrase Winston Churchill: "Democracy is a terrible form of government, but there is none better." DBS is not ideal, but it provides more flexibility than most other systems.

Creating satisfying individual expectations is not easy. It takes a joint effort between the expatriate manager and his or her supervisor. Ideally, the focus is in the best interest of the company, not the individuals.

*Step 6: Maintain continuity of home office support and raise the visibility new career opportunities for expats overseas.*

It takes extra effort to maintain continuity with the home office when an employee is overseas. For this reason, seriously consider sponsoring the employee communities suggested earlier. They serve as an attractive way to maintain links from the home office to the expatriates overseas.

There are even better ways to stay in touch, and maintain personal links with your expats. You can do so by establishing an Ombudsman Office. And you can help further by providing informal networks of personal contacts which, of course, are invaluable. Your most effective open channels of communications are likely social meetings or discussions about organizational changes and career opportunities at "home."

With success in China, you will have not only a bigger business base, but also a bigger "headache": A need for more management attention, and for giving repatriated employees new, substantial assignments. If your China assignments fail, there is little growth opportunity in managing China assignments in your home office. Repatriated employees will need new assignments.

**Managing Your Expats**

Meanwhile, you still must develop a plan for managing your two expat types: Those looking to return home, and those who don't. You will need different management tools for each.

With those looking to return, you can encourage their participation in online communities. In addition, you can provide a home office mentor (or use an Ombudsman Office for problem-solving)–but each step should expand your channels of communications.

For those preferring to stay overseas, you can create a revolving door policy for employees with overseas assignments. This greatly facilitates their transition from one assignment to another. A more radical version of this is Bechtel's: Employees bid for projects on their own. Your company culture may well determine which step you take.

Under normal circumstances, **an effective intranet of job postings**, monitored by HR and augmented by informal networks (developed from online communities) might well work. If your China expatriates find out about opportunities, they can check with HR as well as the informal networks. The burden of career development for any individual reverts back to the expatriate as s/he competes for new assignments (assuming the appropriate skills have been developed for the new assignment).

You should know that there is a vital role for informal networks in China, as there is in the US. The "informal networks" in Western societies are the "Guanxi" of China. In both instances, successful managers learn to perform by tapping large and deep networks–and those using "Guanxi" do the same.

With imperfections in the process, candidates with strong credentials such as Mark Chen can be recruited through executive search firms, or through business community research. To retain Mark, however, requires an attractive work environment with career development potential, a supportive team, and open channels of communication.

> Two further examples of staff selection worth studying are available in the ASH Conglomerate case (*Case #3*) and the ABC Printing Company case (*Case #5*). There, Mark Chen began in the US home office, delivered as required overseas, and stayed linked to the company cultures before and during his "tour." Chen set up profitable businesses, but ASH Conglomerate failed to sustain them when Mark left and settled for "flat-line" performance. The ABC Printing Company reverted back to losses after it failed to create a management team that could retain or replace Mark.

Recruiting overseas for China assignments is more complex, with less chance of success. The D Conglomerate (*Case #2*) was successful in training and developing its Policy Deployment culture in China, but its ability to commit resources for assessing China opportunities depended largely on home office support. T Conglomerate (*Case #1*) was a different situation, as the lack of acquisition capital sparked many issues that focused on quarterly earnings and cash flow.

*Step 7: Prime the ground for overseas "tours" with a strong succession plan, preferably by developing and coaching local talent.*

One core principle in this book: You enjoy the biggest profits when you have capable local talent managing your China operation. You need strong expats to launch the operation; but you need local talent to sustain it.

Companies with a large presence in China like Motorola have vigorous localization programs, yet their business plans continue to use expatriates on the ground in China–with no replacements by local talent. General Motors has an international rotational program for expatriates, and there is a vigorous component localization program for their suppliers, as in most major foreign automotive players in China (e.g., Volkswagen, Ford, etc).

Let's consider some more lessons from our case studies:

> For *ASH Conglomerate* (*Case #3*), Mark Chen developed local talent to replace him, so he was ready for the next assignment. But fellow teammates in his chain of command were unfocused on people development. Result: More turnovers in both line management and HR functions after the Chinese partner reacted strongly to Mark's departure–and thwarted the prospects of expanding the partnership relationship.

> In *the ABC Printing case* (*Case #5*), One manager effectively blocked the communication channels to the home office (hoping to be first choice in the succession plan to replace Mark Chen). Such counterproductive behavior has direct, personal impact on employees with overseas assignments. In short, the trust felt in the company seems violated. In ABC's case (*Case #5*), more expatriates were introduced to the Chinese operations. Result: Risks associated with the company have increased dramatically, and the company no longer sees profits in China.

*Step 8: When appropriate, repatriate your China-based expats, and show how their overseas experience is part of a successful career path in your home office. Champion these career paths as steps that are vital to your company's growth domestically and globally.*

Since excellent employees were recruited for your China assignments, how you handle their repatriation is very important to avoid turnover. Unfortunately, the turnover rates traditionally are very high.

There are few successful repatriation examples. The best ones appear to be in Europe where, for instance, one large power equipment manufacturer *promotes* expats after successful Chinese assignments. This company knows that this action attracts superior candidates year in and year out to China, and they help accelerate profitable growth everywhere.

Consider also the testimony of Leigh Shields, President of Consulting Services of Healthy Companies International, and a US expat who returned from Europe when he was a Vice President of Human Resources with Xerox. Shields emphasizes that "**the key to gaining a sound return on investment is strong repatriation planning.**"

Other repatriation programs include the international rotational programs in General Motors, or the project bidding process at Bechtel.

The key point, after all is said and done: Repatriation is a critical process, important to the success of your company and that of your expat managers and staffers. Give it the attention it so richly deserves.

*Great things are done by a series of small things brought together.*

*—Vincent van Gogh*

# CHAPTER 3
# WORKSHEET

1.  My assessment of the eight-step framework in my company for motivating expats:

    |                                     | Poor | Average | Excellent |
    | ----------------------------------- | ---- | ------- | --------- |
    | • Perform Market Research           | ____ | ____    | ____      |
    | • Allocate Team Resources           | ____ | ____    | ____      |
    | • Establish Market Expectations     | ____ | ____    | ____      |
    | • Select Employees                  | ____ | ____    | ____      |
    | • Customize individual expectations | ____ | ____    | ____      |
    | • Sustain home office support       | ____ | ____    | ____      |
    | • Establish succession plan         | ____ | ____    | ____      |
    | • Implement successful repatriation | ____ | ____    | ____      |

2.  Which Selection Criterion is more important to me:

    a.  Technical experts interested in China business and culture _____

    b.  Strong coaches interested in developing local talent _____

3.  I identify the pool of candidates for overseas assignments by:

    a.  Relying on Human Resources _____

    b.  Working with an interested employee community _____

    c.  Empowering functional supervisors to seek strong candidates _____

    d.  Others (specify) _____

4. My biggest headache in identifying well-qualified candidates for expatriate assignment is:

a. Cost and related benefits _____

b. Communicating the importance of overseas assignments _____

c. Others (specify) _____

5. My biggest headache retaining well-qualified expatriates after their assignment is:

a. Where to put them in the organization _____

b. Having HR find appropriate assignment for them _____

c. Others (specify) _____

Key issues I see in recruiting and developing your expatriates:

_____

_____

*It is one of the most beautiful compensations of this life that
no man can sincerely try to help another without helping himself.*

*—Ralph Waldo Emerson*

# Chapter 4

# Compensation and incentive plans

<u>Note</u>

### *Executive Summary*

- *Your* **incentive compensation is a smaller part** *of your total compensation plan, so motivating expatriates requires long term commitment strengthened by stock options, plus other factors like support for a suitable lifestyle.*

- *Remember:* **Startups of operations depend less on structure**, *more on scheduling and project management. But structure is vital for the long-haul, including a serious focus on compensation plans.*

- *For optimal results,* **ensure you include non-financial incentives** *that include career planning, alongside your financial incentives.*

**American business pioneer Cornelius Vanderbilt** once claimed that the secret to business success was, "Never tell anyone what you're going to do til you've done it." **That simply won't work these days**, and it won't work especially in recruiting people for China-based operations.

We should motivate expats through incentive compensation, and make it clear during the recruiting phase. Yet given the size of typical incentive "comp packages," about 10-15% of an expat's total compensation, current plans undershoot the levels needed.

To bolster your comp plan, and get the most from your expatriates, you must focus long and hard on their long-term career development.

Here's what that means: Rather than ignoring incentive compensation, you use it but understand its limitations. And you focus on

- Elements of an expatriate compensation package
- Maintaining or supporting a suitable lifestyle
- Motivating the expatriate

**Keys to an expatriate compensation package**

At leading businesses, you will find different policies and procedures for compensating the expats. In US companies, there are some standard benefits for all employees:

- 5 year vesting of pension
- Insurance for the family
  - Medical
  - Dental
  - Life Insurance (e.g. for traveling on company business)
- Retirement Accounts (e.g., 401(k))
- Stock purchasing plans—in many cases

The typical US expatriate senior manager package consists of:

| | Avg. US Expatriate[30] |
|---|---|
| Base Salary/Medical/Life Insurance | US$120,000 |
| Incentive Compensation | US$ 40,000 |
| Stock Options | Unrealized value |
| Housing | US$ 50,000 |
| Education | US$ 20,000 per child |
| Transportation/home leave | US$ 20,000 |
| Chinese Taxes    (above US taxes) | US$ 20,000 |

**Note**

| | |
|---|---|
| Relocation | US$ 20,000 |
| US Tax Equalization/Preparation | US$ 30,000 |
| (Optional) Clubs | US$ 10,000 |
| Typical Compensation (2 children) | US$350,000 |

Some offer special benefits for expats specifically to stimulate interest for work sites outside major Chinese cities. These benefits include:

- Hardship allowance
- Location premium

One fact is certain: Base salary and incentive compensation vary significantly from company to company, and by employee rank. Stock Options are available to most employees. Typical housing costs extend up to US$150,000 (US$250,000 in Hong Kong), and there are residences at that level today, but not usually. Education expenses are holding steady, though rising a bit. As for taxes: The top marginal income tax rate in China is 45% (above US levels), but it's lower than in some parts of Europe. Relocation costs depend on the company allowance, family size and length of the assignment. US tax equalization and preparation costs depend on the rest of the package, and club membership sometimes is a business expense instead of an employee benefit.

And some remain discretionary expenses. Example: Housing expenses vary a great deal (by city, size and type of home). There is no single standard, so in the end, it's up to you to decide what's appropriate.

Whatever you do, **avoid the Cornelius Vanderbilt tactic of "hiding" your plan. Keep details crystal clear for your employees**.

To avoid issues, many companies now offer two payments:

- Periodic incentive compensation (usually annually/quarterly), and
- Base salary/housing/education/transportation (typically monthly).

Relocation is often handled separately, and there often is professional tax preparation assistance in many cases.

## Providing Suitable Lifestyles

For a company, the major issue surrounding expats is how to stimulate a supportive family environment while the expatriate focuses on delivering results. In cities outside Shanghai, Beijing, and Guangzhou, the living environment is much more difficult. Some assignments allow the family to live in a different city to accommodate the children's education. This is not an optimal situation–after all, the family remains separated–and you incur higher expenses.

For the individual expat, the real issue is a suitable lifestyle–one that provides for family time and family connection as well as rewarding work.

Key: Focus on the time needed to deliver results. And work to minimize family separation, so that your expats are driven to deliver results, and to be reunited with their families. By focusing on delivery of results (rather than cost savings), your China-based operation will benefit through lower turnover, plus faster and enhanced profitability.

We'll cover similar work-life balance issues in *Chapter 5*.

## Motivating Your Expatriates

In *Chapter 3*, you learned that two expatriate recruiting criteria are cultural sensitivity and effective coaching skills to develop local talent. While this involves some difficulties, our *Case #3*–Mark Chen in ASH Conglomerate–shows the steps needed.

One motivational lesson from Mark Chen's case: Growing companies can expand the expat manager's responsibility–thereby changing the job scope. In turn, the expatriate manager becomes accountable for the performance of the business over a longer period of time.

So **non-financial incentives have impact** on your employees.

The key ingredient in motivating: **Create long-term commitment** between your company and your expatriates. As your company invests significant resources on the business, your expatriates also invest their trust in the organization by putting their career prospects on the line. Violate this trust, and you break the link between the two.

So work to strengthen the link, through long term compensation such as stock options. And work to keep the trust for the long haul. Most expatriates recognize that organizations evolve and change and, therefore, are willing to support improvements. If both entities focus on process improvements, you have win-win results, and build enriching overseas assignments as well as refreshed company culture and brand equity.

**The Main Start-Up and Ongoing Incentives**

Incentive "comp targets" are different for the two types of operations, start-up operations versus ongoing operations. Start-up operations generally have less structure, focusing more on project implementation. Overall, the key components for all incentive comp plans are

- Start up timeline (for startup operations only)
- Budgeting, sales, costs, profits and cash flow
- Team building and resources
- Business development
- Processes training and targets
- Awards, certifications and community activities
- Ethics and compliance guidelines
- Transition and succession plan

Only parts of the above are vital for everyone, but most incentive plans focus purely on financial performance versus budget (sales, etc.). This can drive your operations in counterproductive directions.

Instead, consider how you can maximize benefits from each of these components.

**Start up timeline incentives**

To evaluate performance you need to reach agreement with your expats on the startup timeline, identifying milestones, resources and completion dates. A typical set of milestones is presented in Exhibit 4-1.

**Exhibit 4-1**
**Typical Milestones for Startup Operations in China**

| | Responsible Party | | |
| --- | --- | --- | --- |
| | Company | Partner/ Govt. | New Entity |
| Completion of Market Study | ✓ | | |
| Review Market Study for execution steps | ✓ | | |
| Key Parameters to Control in process | ✓ | | |
| Identification of prospective partners | ✓ | | |
| Letter of Intent signed (if appropriate) | ✓ | ✓ | |
| Project Proposal Completed | | ✓ | |
| Business Plan/Model review/approved | ✓ | | |
| Feasibility Study Completed | | ✓ | |
| Site Selection | ✓ | ✓ | |
| Environmental Study Completed | ✓ | ✓ | |
| Selection of Board members | ✓ | ✓ | |
| Business License | ✓ | ✓ | |
| Initial Board Meeting | ✓ | ✓ | |
| Top Management Team in place | ✓ | ✓ | |
| Funding Approval | ✓ | | |
| Initial Funding | ✓ | ✓ | |
| Recruit/Training for new entity employees | | | ✓ |
| Purchase/Install equipment | | | ✓ |
| Quality Assurance | | | ✓ |
| Initial Systems in place | | | ✓ |
| Operating Permits Obtained | | | ✓ |
| Customer Orders | | | ✓ |
| First Sales | | | ✓ |
| First Profit Dollar | | | ✓ |
| First Profitable Year | | | ✓ |
| Additional Systems in place | | | ✓ |

Many milestones are not entirely controllable by an individual. Some approval processes must happen within a specified timeframe. Additional Board meetings and funding events all happen within this timeframe.

**Note**

Once you recruit your expatriates, you must deliver the right resources to achieve the milestones. An inadequate team or poor funding make progress difficult. So especially if you're starting with a big project, make the transitioning "out" of expatriates in a startup a vital issue, and devote the right resources to this "transient" phase in your future operations.

After all, **you want an auspicious–not a rocky–start**, don't you?

**Budget benchmarks and related financial incentives**

After the startup, your expats will offer financial projections and discuss targets and short-term priorities. The projections include budgeted sales, costs and cash flow.

Budgeted sales projections must be linked to commissions available to sales people, plus agreement on performance evaluations of sales support personnel (e.g., engineering, customer service). Keep these revenue projections realistic, if you want to drive performance, instead of politics.

As for costs, most foreign entities remain relatively small in China (exceptions include Motorola). In the cost details, you generally find a few large entries reflecting "corporate allocations" or "allocated expenses," and this may include expatriate expenses. Usually, this large figure is often ignored as "uncontrollable," leaving little flexibility for other important expenses such as training and development.

Discretion, as you know, plays a large role in special initiatives like a China based operation. Your China-based senior manager has fiduciary responsibilities to the home company. But that manager still senses split loyalties–between the new China-based enterprise (as top manager) and the home office (as employee). Try to manage this delicate balance here with empathy.

Use one guiding principle: Remind everyone that the home office is the investor, and the China-based enterprise is its operating arm. If the operating arm finds an attractive opportunity to pursue, try to ensure that it makes the "case" for the expected return on investment. In other words, ensure the opportunity is attractive to "investor" and "operations arm" alike. Your channel of communication will be the approval of the minutes of the Board of Directors for the China-based enterprise.

Now in fact, this is **a case of "easy to say, and hard to do."**

For example, you need to help your "operating arm" understand the cost-benefit of "allocated expenses." One tradeoff to discuss is the tradeoff involving and excluding expatriates. The priorities will surface quickly.

And if you want continuous improvement in your "operations arm," try "accelerating" the learning of your China-based employees. This will also drive bigger savings. As the "operations arm" tackles the weak points in your operations, you drive down costs. Use this tactic in negotiating with advertisers, distributors, and suppliers. Among your own costs, you can find material and labor savings to offset new business costs and research costs for finding new opportunities.

In short, you can keep costs low, and profits higher via established improvement processes, e.g., Six Sigma. It's impossible to create these processes out of a vacuum. So spend some time with your expats setting up realistic expectations, with realistic assessments.

Many budgets, of course, are set by upper echelon, and passed through to their expatriate managers.

One solution is to use organizational structure, if it's appropriate. The higher the level of your expat organization, the fewer the management layers filtering your budget, and the higher your visibility on issues. Let's illustrate this:

> In the T Conglomerate case (*Case #1*), the management chain is complex: China reports to Hong Kong, and that office reports to Singapore, which itself reports to a Business Unit President who reports to Corporate. Result: It's almost impossible for sales to achieve targets in China without acquisitions. By flattening this kind of structure, you create significant improvement, and unearth many aggressive accounting treatments. The main roots of issues like these reflect company culture. Overall, such cultures are not effective without continuing acquisitions.

In the ASH Conglomerate case (*Case #3*), Mark Chen's JV is profitable but not large enough to make an impact in ASH Conglomerate's financial statements. Main issue: The JV is so deep down the "org structure" that it disappears off the corporate radar, despite generating newsworthy stories for the company.

## Team building and resources incentives

Once the China operation starts up, most of the team is drawn from local Chinese. So team building especially requires substantial cultural sensitivity and patience. The tools: Informal coaching and training by the company "road warriors" and expatriates–plus any documentation (e.g., manuals) that are translated. In this situation, annual "360 degree surveys"–evaluating expats' performance as seen by supervisors, peers, and subordinates–can usefully assess team building effectiveness.

Critical to the team building: Knowing where to focus to achieve the biggest impact. Here, you can always tap a simple fact. Most China-based employees are familiar with the gaps in the team's capabilities; now you need to prioritize your resources to fill the gaps[24]. Ask your expats to describe the gaps, the resources needed and how their gaps can be filled? Their responses provide a strong signal of how well your expatriates are ready to prioritize resources–and deliver performance.

## Business development incentives

Your core competence reflects capabilities that often have high value in China but low value at "home." A typical example is a strong Information Technology process well documented to facilitate transactions. These latent skills may form the beginning of a local skills base that sustains profitable growth in China (in Phase 5 of the *Business Life Cycle*).

Example from the Genteli Telecom case (*Case #4*): Here, a Geographic Information System is on hand to establish line-of-sight for creating a wireless network. But the system can also be used by architectural engineers. With Internet advances and the emerging strong broadband infrastructure in China, these opportunities can create important competitive advantages.

You can discuss these opportunities with your expatriates as part of the performance evaluation.

**Quality process training and targets**

Quality processes are key tools for transferring management or technical skills. Let's consider one example:

> In our ASH Conglomerate case (*Case #3*), one key to Mark Chen's success was the training of the Chinese workforce in the US. Armed with basic skills, the Chinese employees observed how the process in the US translated into productivity. This created a paradigm shift, and was transferred to the Chinese operation, creating process improvement that is unique to China.
>
> The Chinese JV delivered higher productivity than the US operations within six months of start-up.

All subsequent productivity improvements serve as monitoring tools for evaluating your progress in localizing operations.

**Awards, certifications and outreach**

Responsible corporate citizens in a Chinese community build brand equity, employee loyalty, and develop "Guanxi" with the Chinese government. Consider this example:

> In our ABC Printing Company case (*Case #5*), the operation achieved the "High Technology Enterprise" level partly because it demonstrated new uses of print content through cellular phones, and through sponsorship of local community events. **NOTE:** The "High Technology Enterprise" designation–in fact, a "certification" by the government-translates into millions of dollars of tax savings once the company becomes profitable.

You and your team can discuss which certifications are crucial. But to extract even more value from these, publicize the achievements as a way to monitor your progress toward localizing operations.

### Ethical and compliance issues

If you underline one thing in this book, make it this point: **Do not compromise your integrity**. The strength of your operations may be hard for your company to gauge, especially if your company communication channels are blocked. Do listen to your team, and make decisions about what is acceptable when tricky ethical issues surface. One touchstone: Ask yourself, "Is this the right thing to do?" If yes, do it.

You have some tools to help. In the US, the "Foreign Corrupt Practices Act" allows prosecution of corrupt individuals. Employees subject to its reach cannot hide behind a corporate fig leaf.

Unfortunately, only some acts fall under the umbrella notion of "corruption." So rely on your own ethical strengths and your team's to guide you. Your reward for doing this: You keep your reputation intact.

The key: The marketplace is competitive, and many short-sighted players will surface. They lack staying power, and lose once their unethical behaviors are uncovered. Good business people generally agree that, in the long run, people get what they deserve. (Of course, as economist John Maynard Keynes pointed out, "In the long run, we'll all dead.")

Regardless of size, your company should weigh carefully whether to pursue short term profit at the risk of exposing the company to scandal, and worse, prosecution. In the event of unethical "moves" (intentional or not), the company suffers, and is held accountable through lost future opportunities. Consider this example from one of our case studies:

> In the T Conglomerate case (*Case #1*), incentive compensation plans are driving aggressive accounting practices. The expats in China say they're only doing as they're directed to do. And they vigorously block inquiries about their business practices. As the Chinese might say, the expatriates are like babies too big for their cribs. If the regional office supports them, it will take time to change the culture even with transparent financial reporting.

### Timeline for transition and succession plans

You have to start succession planning for expatriates even before their expatriation. Why? This plan impacts the success of your expatriates.

It is vital to demonstrate to your expatriates that you are serious about supporting them, and equally serious about maintaining continuity in your China-based operations. So prepare to publicize your successful repatriations. **Establish within your company's communications that China assignments help build personal career paths**.

At stake is the ultimate success of your China-based business. Time spent communicating how well your expats fare after repatriation has its own reward: You will have a continuing stream of new, solid recruits.

*One of the secrets of life is*
*to make stepping stones out of stumbling blocks.*

*—Jack Penn*

# CHAPTER 4
# WORKSHEET

1. I spend $ _____/year on ____ (#) of US and ____ (#) of Hong Kong/Taiwan expatriates to manage $_____ in sales in China.

2. The average incentive component of the compensation package is ____% of the base pay, or ____% of the total compensation package.

3. My incentive compensation plan includes the following elements:
   a. Startup schedule (if applicable)          ____%
   b. Budget sales/cost/profit/cash flow        ____%
   c. Team building resources             ____%
   d. Business development               ____%
   e. Processes/training and targets        ____%
   f. Awards/certifications/community services   ____%
   g. Ethical/compliance                  ____%
   h. Transition/succession plan          ____%

                                          Total    100 %

4. China is ____ layers of reporting from corporate HQ, and reports to:
   a. Greater China (Hong Kong or Taiwan)     ____
   b. North or East Asia                   ____
   c. Asia                                ____
   d. Europe                         ____

   e.  Home Office (in US/Europe/Australia)     ____

   f.  Others (specify_____)     ____

5.  How do our comp packages compare to my competitors/peers/customers/suppliers?

   ____ Above Average      ____ About the same      ____ Below Average

Key issues I see in compensation and incentive plans:

_____

_____

_____

*People talk about the middle of the road as though it were unacceptable. Actually, all human problems, excepting morals, come into the gray areas. Things are not all black and white. There have to be compromises. The middle of the road is all of the usable surface. The extremes, right and left, are in the gutters.*

—Dwight D. Eisenhower

## Chapter 5

# Work-life balance in China-clubs, schools and religion

Note

### *Executive Summary*

- **Expatriates and their families have different needs** *which must be addressed to maximize productivity from your key China-based investment–whether it involves $millions or $billions.*

- *To help your expats,* **target 3 areas to unite expatriate families** *on foreign soil: Clubs, schools and religious communities–all vital to establishing the right work-life balance.*

- **Expats in cities like Shanghai, Beijing and Guangzhou** *require special attention–because of the significantly different living conditions outside these population centers.*

**What does "work-life balance" mean to you?** What should it mean to expatriates who will operate 12-13 time zones away from your "HQ"?

76

For expatriates and their families, their "burning issue" is a need to focus sharply on performance, without burning out, and without sacrificing family time excessively.

To help them, your company needs to

- **Help expatriates deliver results** to their stakeholders: customers, suppliers, partners and employees–while you…

- **Offer the expatriates families rewarding experiences** so they support (rather than distract from) the breadwinner's focus.

As you will see, 3 institutions can help you achieve this. These help unite expat families, and link them to the home office community. They are:

1. Clubs

2. International schools

3. Religious groups, especially churches

Let's consider see how these can support your China initiatives by first examining the **needs of expatriate employees** and **their spouses.**

### The Needs of Expatriates, Your First Stakeholders

*How can expatriates find information* about their customers, suppliers, and partners? Chambers of Commerce are the best place to start.

In 2002, the US Chamber of Commerce (AmCham) represented over 3 million businesses, with 92 AmChams abroad. There are seven AmChams in Greater China[31], and many European Chambers. Some are better organized to help expatriates than others. Not surprisingly, the cities with AmCham are generally more advanced commercial cities with superior infrastructure (airports and roads). The AmChams here generally have a wealth of information, and are excellent reference sources for supplementing internal company resources.

However, if your operations are outside the cities with AmChams, life quickly turns difficult. For expats traveling extensively throughout China, the significant variation in quality of transport can impact productivity.

> **Example**: Take the Hong Kong-to-Shenzhen train around the holidays, and you get a vivid image of "wall to wall people." At other times, air travel inside China still pales in comparison with air travel in North America, Europe or Australia. Airports often operate on Visual Flight Rules (VFR). When aircraft are delayed, the schedule for the rest of the day is usually delayed, since the concept of having "spare" aircraft to accommodate flight delays is still far from mature.

**A significant issue: Meeting times**. Due to lack of control rather than planning, scheduling meetings in China is difficult, especially if you plan many meetings with lots of travel in between. This is a key driver for the thriving cellular phone businesses in China.

> China leads the rest of the world in cell phone usage. Already the world's largest market (200 million cell phones), China's market is still growing, as Motorola rolls out new Chinese-designed cell phones. The life of a cell phone in China is also shorter than that of the US, inviting an attractive replacement market.

Chinese do things differently–whether they're replacing cell phones, or talking on cell phones. Example: Chinese business people interrupt conversations and take calls, while Americans turn off their cell phones during conversations. And while Americans are increasingly restricting or banning smoking in public, China is a growth market for tobacco companies. A typical negotiation is held in a roomful of cigarette smoke; as a courtesy, people offer cigarettes to one another. Drinking at meals is almost mandatory in many cities, and many Chinese enjoy Karaoke entertainment.

The lessons here? Typical workdays are stressful to expats, especially if they're motivated to deliver results on a rigid timeline.

**How can you help your expatriates?** Best bet: Learn ways to maintain regular contact with your expatriates, and turn to institutions and groups.

Actual work-life balance for expats may be tough to come by. Try finding expats like Mark Chen–see *Case #3*, on p.42 (above)–two target results and doing the right thing (more on this in *Chapter 6*). Consider how work-life balance issues are resolved in other cases:

> In the ABC Printing case (*Case #5*), Mark Chen spent little time with family, and despite 5-hour daily commutes and a big workload, trained his workforce after doing time-and-motion studies on all functions. He often worked the second and third shifts. His local club membership was useful only to meet customers, close sales transactions and training.

> As for the T Conglomerate (*Case #1*), Mark Chen averaged under 10 days monthly in Shanghai (his base of operations), constantly traveling to see staff, HQ and customers. He built a local team of managers to monitor and manage the transition and increased transparency in financial reporting. This became mission critical because aggressive accounting practices were becoming harmful to employees and unsustainable for the long term. He was unable to take full advantage of his AmCham membership.

> Perhaps the most remarkable travel story was in ASH Conglomerate (*Case #3*) when, during a 15 month span between 1994 and 1995, Mark Chen averaged about 80 hours monthly in the air during negotiations and start-up phases of his JV.

> The full "picture" here:
> - Customer and partner were in Shanghai;
> - Chinese government approval authorities, in Beijing;
> - US FAA government certification authorities, in Singapore;
> - ASH's Asian Corporate HQ, in Hong Kong;

- Aerospace Asian Headquarters, in Tokyo;
- Aerospace Global Headquarters, in California;
- Aircraft Landing Systems business unit, in Indiana; and
- ASH Conglomerate HQ remained in New Jersey.

Strategies set in Indiana were reviewed in Tokyo and Hong Kong, as negotiations were held in Shanghai, before Chinese government approval in Beijing, ASH's approval in California and New Jersey, plus US Government certification approval in Singapore. (Training of the start-up's workforce was held in Pennsylvania and Arizona.)

The outcomes: This was ASH's one profitable investment in China for five years. The profitable JV was so success-ful, in fact, that it was featured on the cover of ASH Conglomerate's 1995 Annual Report. But few "lessons learned" were captured or used by ASH.

## The Needs of the Spouse

What does the spouse of an expatriate do after landing in China? The excitement of being among local Chinese fades within weeks after arrival. After finding new friends, they have to find productive activities. Other than children (and schools), typical activities are working (for pay or as volunteer), exercis-ing, eating, going to religious groups or traveling. Exercising and meeting friends are two staple activities.

China does not accommodate expat families easily. Outside the "home" (often in secluded expat areas), the streets are crowded. Despite a national government edict by the Chinese govern-ment, Chinese still spit on the streets, dump cigarette butts, and may forget their manners. Plus, southern China (Guangdong Province) has seen several near epidemics in 1997 and 2003. The World Health Organization (WHO) issued an unusual global alert and a special hotline in 2003 to monitor a new virus known as Severe Acute Respiratory Syndrome (SARS). Thousands of cases have been identified in at least 20 countries with an overall 8-15% mortality rate.[1]

The next traveler's vignettes may be rare in Shanghai, but can be part of your experience in rural areas. And your experiences may depend on your ability to speak some Chinese.

For English speakers arriving at an airport, drivers will pursue you to offer rides. They first offer a low fare to your destination. But when you arrive, the fare suddenly quadruples. You're charged for each luggage piece, or for each kilometer, or for unfamiliar units of measure. If you refuse to pay, you still must take time to extricate yourself from the situation. (In fairness, this can still happen in Miami or New York, too.)

For Chinese (Mandarin) speakers: If you're on a bicycle and someone gets knocked down, don't bother apologizing unless you prefer being cursed and criticized for some time. The "street rules" of etiquette call for yelling at the other party, even if the yeller is at fault. After a crowd gathers and offers its opinion, everyone eventually disperses, and you'll soon enough be on your way.

For Shanghaiese speakers: Unless you shop at new hyper-markets (Carrefour), street vendors will listen for your Shanghaiese accent, and adjust their pricing. Avoid making requests that begin with "Please…": Your price instantly rises above "market rate." But if you ask bluntly "how much?" you may get the real price–if your Shanghaiese accent sounds legitimate to vendors' ears.

## Key Issues and Community-Based Solutions

Expats who travel extensively will find that their spouses face tough times in cities without strong foreign communities. One solution: Use the available religious group or church for spiritual and emotional support. (For the **role of religious groups**, see p. 84 below.)

The core idea: Companies that help the spouse help themselves. A spouse without additional support will turn to your expat manager–not the best solution if you want your expat focused on tackling work issues.

In addition, expats face some tough ethical issues.

> **A sensitive issue: The use of products in violation** of intel-lectual property rights. There are many inexpensive Rolexes. Good quality new DVD movies now cost under US$3 each. As noted in our "Engaging your counterparts" section, these problems may be driven by Westerners' his-toric disrespect for China for over a century (through 1949), and remains the topic of many books[32, 33]. As a result, it affects the work-life balance ledger, since you must make decisions after establishing a "line in the sand" in this area. It may be enough to say this: There are few Western-style movie theaters, and many expat families have collections of DVDs–so they watch these as they spend family time together.

**Schools and Children**

Remember: The siting of expat assignments determines the quality of schools available to their families. Due to language barriers, expatriate kids generally mix poorly with local students and, instead, the parents make efforts to send them to interna-tional schools. The well-established international schools are found in Guangzhou, Shanghai, and Beijing.

*Quality of schooling*–While not a comprehensive measure of quality, in a typical year more students from Beijing International School apply to Princeton University (one of the most competitive undergraduate institutions) than Guangzhou and Shanghai American Schools combined. In Shanghai, you find 7 international schools and 14 kindergartens listed in Shanghai's 2002-2003 AmCham Directory. The Shanghai American School is by far the most popular school for Americans, with over a thousand students on two campuses. Beyond Shanghai, the pattern of availability and quality of the international schools is similar to that of AmCham.

*After-school activities*–Few after-school options exist for kids out-side the international schools. While there are special field trips (camping in Malaysia, volleyball in Japan), the daily staple after school means computer games and more computer games. Rising in popularity recently, especially in Shanghai, is youth soccer. An international school league has started play in Shanghai, but few Chinese cities have such soccer leagues.

The result: The children of expats need more attention as they grow older. As in Western societies, High-School aged adolescent students are bolder in testing limits. Some suffer serious consequences like pregnancies; others might be engaged in hooliganism–shooting BB guns at bicyclists–and wind up being jailed by police.

How do you make your expatriate families feel "at home" in China? Let's review 3 institutions that help make expatriate families' lives closer to those in their home country. The institutions are clubs, international schools, and religious groups (and churches).

## Role of Social Clubs

Many social clubs provide an environment for expats and local executives who want sanctuaries away from the daily grind. Some clubs are prestigious and offer many amenities. Others focus on dining and a relaxed experience, and still others target physical fitness.

We strongly recommend you provide (or seek out) access to one or more of these clubs. For expats, these are excellent settings in which to do business. For families, these sites offer ways to relax in more comfortable surroundings. Family stress, remember, significantly impacts the productivity of expats. And there are tradeoffs: Club memberships can pay for themselves by higher productivity if expats are better motivated to deliver results.

In Shanghai, expatriates have organized sports events. These include Ultimate Frisbee games, "Hairy Crab" Rugby teams that compete internationally, and informal golf and tennis matches. Except for golf outings, these are the least expensive "club" sports.

Beware: Club membership costs vary significantly. You have discretion on what to offer expatriates. If you want loyal and productive employees, the investment is worth it. For companies that pay lump sum compensation and include benefits, this is an employee decision.

Your challenge: Maintain a steady focus on delivering results. You want to satisfy the expatriate on assignment, and help him focus on results–and not on uncomfortable living conditions.

## International Schools

For many students, the quality of education is good. In the case of some expatriates, there is a good chance that the children are gifted and talented (as the label is used in the United States).

So there may be issues. For gifted and talented students, international schools may be sub-optimal learning environments. One solution is to have the child skip a grade, but it exposes the child to older kids. This is risky: Some kids lack the discipline and social skills needed to focus on schoolwork. The brightest students often require significant parental support to succeed.

Roots of frustration with schooling vary. One frustration for bright kids derives from different levels of English comprehension in the classrooms. In typical international schools, 10 nationalities are represented, and English is not a native tongue for all students. At times, the teaching pace is reconfigured, the delivery of course material slowed down, and the class then begins to address the needs of those struggling to keep up.

Turnover is another source of issues. Many international school students are in school briefly, then leave when their parents leave. Few students remain in an international school for consecutive years since expatriate turnover is high. So schools find it difficult to develop curricula for all students–and must wait until the last minute (when students are confirmed). In this kind of environment, expatriate children may think it easier to test limits and try to "get away" with bad behavior. After all, they know they will not be around very long. "Rootlessness"–whether among military or expatriate families–takes its toll on children, and the maturity required to handle that is difficult to come by.

## Religious Groups and Churches

The discussion immediately below focuses on spiritual support available to Protestants and Catholics (the dominant religious affiliations of China-based expats). But it must be pointed out that Jews and Chinese are traditional friends, in part because Shanghai was one of the few "safe harbors" for Jews seeking refuge during World War II[34]. The synagogue that stood during World War II still thrives today in Shanghai.

Given our unscientific survey, it appears there are more Protestant Christians than Catholics among the Chinese expatriate community. Among the local Chinese, it's clear that there is more of a balance between Protestants and Catholics. The evidence: The Pope has established an important reporting relationship for his Bishop in China, in part to reflect the somewhat large Catholic population within China. In Shanghai, the Catholic Church occupies an impressive older building, while Protestants began to congregate in a rental church only in the mid-1990s, after accepting a government agreement that their sermons include a local Chinese preacher preaching in English.

Prior to this government agreement, protestant Christians assembled in hotels, and were officially prevented from assembling in a church pending the arrangement for a Chinese preacher. Beyond the church, there are also many Bible study groups, Christian fellowship meetings, retreats and activities organized by the expatriate Christian community.

**One topic remains an issue for the government**. The Chinese government still keeps local Chinese separated from expatriates in Sunday church services. Shanghai services for local Chinese are conducted in the morning. The same services for expatriates, with a Chinese priest delivering a sermon in English and an expatriate priest delivering a similar sermon, are held in the afternoon. In this environment, it remains clear that expatriates should avoid trying to convert local Chinese to Christianity–and this is important since some expats may be forceful Evangelical Christians.

Christians and their churches, in addition, play a major role in disaster relief. Christian missions–based in Taiwan or Hong Kong–brought their relief missions to cities like Wuhan in Central China.

Bibles are not officially allowed for sale in China, even though R. R. Donnelley, with a large printing facility in Shenzhen, is the largest Bible printer in the world. Rule of thumb: Protestants and Catholics moving to China should bring their own copies of the Bible. And beware bringing too many copies: Chinese Customs may become suspicious and question your motives and intentions.

Churches, we should add, are important for adults and their Sunday Schools are popular meeting places for children. Christianity has been the source of unity among foreigners, including those expatriates from Taiwan and Hong Kong in China. Churches offer common ground to share common values and experiences. They are "clubs" open to all, and their meetings can be held in expat homes–making housing an important consideration when trying to place an expat family in a home.

Religious considerations aside, companies must still remember the expanse and variations in the Chinese landscape. Shanghai has 17 million people, and most are officially census-registered based on domiciles ("hukuo"). This is comparable to the population of New York State (in the US) or Tokyo in Japan, but little more than 1% of China's entire population. And there are more large cities throughout the country.

The resulting variety of "business experience" these offer can be mind-boggling. Expats working in Shanghai, China's commercial capital, see business life that is unusual elsewhere in China. Beijing, China's cultural capital of China, offers a different set of business practices generally, and the blonde-haired, blue-eyed Chinese in Western China communicating in languages of Islamic peoples (Turkish and Farsi), offer yet a "third way" of doing business in China. In short, the work-life balance issues outside major cities remain major challenges.

**The big lesson for companies priming the ground for a China-based startup: China's opportunities are many; so are its challenges**, especially around work-life balance problems.

As China continues to push business development away from the coastal region, businesses will accelerate their move inland, to areas where the business climate and related business practices are far less mature. The lack of balance in economic development between the inland and coastal regions remains a key concern for the Chinese government, because it can spark social unrest.

All of this is to say that understanding work-life balance issues in China is vital to your China-based operation. These issues impact the success of your expatriates daily, and influence their ability to conduct meetings, make connections between cities, train and coach their local Chinese employees assignments. This is doubly true if your operations arm is based outside the major cities (Shanghai, Beijing, and Guangzhou).

Your one solution: Stay focused on "the road ahead" and pay attention to the terrain. It changes as you drive inward into China, and makes greater demands on your entire Chinese operation. If you want to deliver results in optimal fashion, give your expatriates' families a positive work-life balance, and the expatriates themselves the tools they need to succeed.

*To put the world right in order, we must first put the nation in order.*
*To put the nation in order, we must first put the family in order.*
*To put the family in order, we must first cultivate our personal life,*
*we must first set our hearts right.*

*—Confucius*

# CHAPTER 5
# WORKSHEET

1. In cities like Shanghai, Beijing, Guangzhou, I have _____ expatriate spouses and _____ children who in terms of their living environment, most likely say they are-

   _____Happy            _____Neutral            _____Unhappy

2. Outside the major Chinese business cities, I have _____ expatriate spouses and _____ children who, in terms of their living environment, will probably say they are-

   _____Happy            _____Neutral            _____Unhappy

3. My company's average tenure for expatriates is _____ years. Of these, _____% of the _____ # of expatriates have families living with them overseas.

   These "average tenure" figures are (check one):

   _____ Significantly higher      _____About the same        _____Significantly below…the percentage of my comparably-ranked employees in the home office. This "turnover differential" tells me how my expatriates' population compares to the home office employees.

4. My expatriates are generally in these segments of the Career Life Cycle:

   _____Segment 1      _____Segment 2      _____Segment 3      _____Segment 4

   (0-5 yrs)          (5-20 yrs)          (20-30 yrs)          (30+yrs)

5. On my visits to China, I normally spend the following amounts of time visiting-

    \_\_\_\_ % Customers                 \_\_\_\_% at the local office/factory

    \_\_\_\_ % Employees               \_\_\_\_% at hotels and/or clubs

    \_\_\_\_ % Suppliers                \_\_\_\_% at church

    \_\_\_\_ % Others (_____)         \_\_\_\_ % at (_____)

100 % Total                      100 % Total

The key issues that challenge my company's expatriate "work-life" balance:

_____

_____

_____

*You gain strength, courage and confidence by every experience in which
you really stop to look fear in the face. You are able to say to yourself,
'I have lived through this horror. I can take the next thing that comes along.'
You must do the thing you think you cannot do.*

—*Eleanor Roosevelt (1884-1962)*

## Section III

# Achieve longer-term goals through company culture and strong character

Note

By now you've established your goals and your team on the ground. Is your team delivering as you expected? What might keep it from performing optimally?

Through print media and many other sources, you know you'll face tough ethical temptations in China. The country has an immature court system, an often hard-to-move bureaucracy and quite often, the unscrupulous character or two who will try to offer shortcuts to "business riches" in China.

The cardinal first rule in China business transactions: **Assume the "golden rule" works**, and unfailingly take the "higher road" when facing these many temptations–ethical ones, especially.

Given the range of decisions to be made-whether by expatriates or local managers–you'll do well to keep a second principle in mind. **Do your decision making as you would do it at the home office.** But beware one key hurdle: This is highly dependent on the state of your company culture and company character, adjusted to local market practices.

**"Culture," in its basic meaning, is simply your employees' collective behavior over time.** There are **visible parts** to company culture: You see them in statements of mission, vision, and

91

creeds. The **"hidden"** parts of the culture, on the other hand, comprise informal employee signals, networks, and shared "off the record"[35] values.

And—no surprise—it's these informal networks, driven by individuals, that create the glue that underpins a company's collective **culture** and **character.**

Much has been written about culture, even more about the "character" of individuals, but one things stands out. **"Character" is the inward motivation to do what's right, even when no one is watching** (as the Character First![36] Institute puts it). In short, "strong character" companies select employees with innately high integrity.

So **"culture" reflects the formal and informal communications that define how decision making is done in a company** (how people do what's right when people are watching). **"Character" is the behavior that ensures people do what's right when people aren't watching. Together, they define the moral strength of your employees. And both are vital to your success, especially in China.**

**We've discussed the need to establish goals (Section I), and execute through expatriates (Section II). Let's now help your team set priorities and make decisions that create a healthy culture and strong character—as you would in the home office.**

**We'll consider culture and character as to apply to 3 groups of employees:**

- **Home office expatriates**

  You actually communicate culture when you define the authority and hierarchy of your expatriates. You can try to see through the opaque informal network to take a glimpse at the collective character of your expatriates.

- **Local Chinese employees**

  You can not succeed without local Chinese employees. Studies such as Hewitt Associates' Best Employers of Asia survey[37] are helpful to understand their perspectives.

- <u>Taiwan and Hong Kong expatriates</u>

   These are generally viewed as catalysts for higher growth if properly managed.

**What do you do when you find severe cultural differences between your company and your Chinese partner?** Cultural differences can spell disaster, as the American Motor Company's Jeep joint venture in Beijing[38] demonstrated in the 1990's. (More illustrative cases are found in Carolyn Blackman's excellent *China Business: Rules of the Game*.[39])

**The key is to see the value of healthy culture and character, and to demonstrate its impact, we can correlate these with the practices of "best employers."** We can do this easily with US companies, since it is here that we have sufficient history and plenty of highly-measured employment practices.

**In the highly-regarded Hewitt Associates study of "best employers," we can readily see that these employers consistently outperform the market (measured by 3-year, 5-year, and 10-year returns of the companies in question**[40]**).** If we take simply the 3-year average as a reference, the best companies delivered 32% higher return than the Standard & Poor's (S&P) 500 companies. If we track this through, we see that the best companies deliver consistently higher return at 5 and 10-year measurement points, vs. the S&P.

**Besides rate of return, the Hewitt Associates and Vanderbilt University**[41] **study targeted voluntary turnover, and applications per employee to measure value. Study results: The top 25 companies had 36% lower voluntary turnover rates, 35% more recruiting applications per employee.** In other words, the best companies receive 35% more applications per employee when recruiting, and see 36% fewer openings due to lower voluntary turnover.

**If we use these lessons in planning for expatriates in China, we can actually project a value for improvement through strong cultural and "character"-based practices.** Suffice it to say that you will enjoy lower rates of turnover and gain higher "monetized" (dollar) value in recruiting employees, if your company

**Note**

sticks to strong, time-tested cultural and "character-centric" practices.

Your Chinese operation, of course, will not simply mimic typical US companies. Most Chinese operations averaged US$12 million in annual sales (in 2000), so the size of a typical Chinese operation may be much smaller than the one found one in your home office. In addition, it needs to be "nimbler," and be able to adjust to its local Chinese market environment.

**Just how can your expatriate team help it do that? Start by recognizing that your expatriates are professionals and your principal change agents.** They're on the ground in China to move your company into its next phase. They're not there to become career managers onsite—unless you find a strong business case to support their expenses.

**In addition, you want your expats shifting to select, hire and train local managers—so that the local Chinese can sustain your profitable growth.** Meanwhile, you will be carefully planning out their repatriation.

As much as possible, leave your product localization to your local managers who know how to match your product or service to the Chinese market environment.

**By the end, all these transitions constitute "Thinking Globally, Acting Locally" in the best sense of the idea. And you'll succeed only so long as your expats and local managers together commit to ethical practices, which in turn, help you replicate your home office's culture and "character."**

**This is a good point to take a close-up view of your team.**

*He who walketh with the wise men will be wise.*

*—Proverbs 13:20a*

# Chapter 6

# Healthy Culture and Character

## *Executive Summary*

- **You have 3 types of culture**–*home office, expatriate, and local management–in China with which to attract customers, partners, suppliers and employees.*

- *To sustain profitable growth,* **you want to maintain healthy cultures** *that attract equally healthy* **communities of business counterparts** *(customers, partners, suppliers and employees).*

- **"Strong character" on your team**–*meaning staffers who "do the right things (even) when no one is looking"*–**strengthens every level of culture** *in your China-based operation.*

**Is your culture "transparent" to others?**

Every time you travel to China or host a Chinese delegation at home, you communicate your culture, verbally and in other ways. The question remains: Is it visible to others, and do you want it visible in THIS way?

To understand how your company can do that, consider a political parallel. Let's review how the US and China began to establish diplomatic relations in the 1970s.

The Chinese invited the US ping-pong team to China in 1971, after the Table Tennis World Championship Games in Japan. President Richard Nixon promptly sent Dr. Henry Kissinger to leverage this friendly gesture into more long-term and friendly exchanges. Dr. Kissinger traveled to China before President Nixon flew to Shanghai and signed the Shanghai Communiqué in 1972.

After 7 years of friendly exchanges, President Jimmy Carter (eventually a 2002 Nobel Peace Laureate) finally set up diplomatic relations with China on January 1, 1979.

It's been 24 years since, and the countries now boast US$110 billion in total trade (by 2000), and they're engaged in discussions on many global issues that include the North Korean situation.

The **key to the evolving relationship in these 30 years**: Steady, continued expansion of friendship, linked by win-win solutions. Both sides still test the boundaries of this friendship as they continue to engage each other. Differences remain understood and respected.

**Can political history help your business?** The goals and objectives are different, but the process is instructive to everyone:

- First, our "counterparts," the Chinese offer invitations to "engage."

- Dr. Kissinger, the initial representative, in Career Life Cycle Segment 2 (Note: He becomes Secretary of State only in 1973–after the Shanghai communiqué is signed.)

- Many teams take part in negotiations.

- Checks and balances are put in place to review and approve action steps (e.g., permanent Most Favored Nation trade status is left for approval by the US Congress).

- Progress grows when both focus on areas of cooperation (Asian currency crisis, the North Korea situation) while trying to influence areas of difference (democracy, human rights).

**Compare this process to your parallel "project" process:**

- You identify an important potential market in China.

- You pick expatriates (and supportive "sales road warriors") to drive your growth in a new China-based operation.

- You set up many expat teams to negotiate and manage your growth.

- You set up strong processes, policies, procedures to review and approve resource allocations.

- Meanwhile, you engage Chinese customers, suppliers, partners or employees with shared values so you can lower your risk of your China investments.

Your next steps: **Find your operating "counterpart" community in China**, and confirm that yours is the right team to execute your strategy.

For starters, consider your first step, and its Chinese corollary: **How will anyone know what you offer?** Images of your company can accumulate through meetings, conversations, or comments from third parties (your reputation). That reputation might become a dominant mode for transmitting information about you, since the sheer number of foreign companies can overwhelm your potential China partners. Advertising can increase awareness and enhance your image, but can not establish your reputation. (There are 165,000 Chinese enterprises, but 42 million in US, Europe and Australia). This is an issue that prompts Chinese to take their time learning what's important about you.

On your side, you know that reputation is important to every business transaction. It directly impacts who is attracted to **your "counterpart community" of customers, suppliers, partners and employees.**

As we discussed earlier (*Chapters 3-5*), motivated employees in mid-career (Career Life Cycle Segments 2-3) are best suited to deliver results for you. Your challenge: Now motivate them to create a healthy culture.

Two more factors are vital to a successful culture in China:

- **You remain–for the long term–a role model for how the Chinese will participate in the global business community.**

  To help the Chinese adopt international trade rules, you must maintain high integrity. What you do is emulated by your counterpart community (customers, suppliers, partners and employees).

- **Your own behavior will be remembered long and well.**

  Chinese have long memories. They still treat Dr. Kissinger as a VIP in China. But this remains a two-edged sword. Rectifying ethics breaches, for example, is painful and difficult because of the "long Chinese memory." So it's crucial to establish your ethical reputation as soon as possible, and maintain it.

The most tangible part of your company culture is your decision making, and its "hierarchical backup." You communicate your culture whenever you delegate decisions and authority to expatriate managers. So the clearest way to establish your healthy culture is to set up multiple channels of open communications with your entire counterpart community–that is, all customers, suppliers, partners and employees.

**Your task at this point**: Make them aware of your decision process.

Different organizations have different structures that define decision making and their culture in China. In our case studies:

| *Case Study* | *Entity/person "managing" China* |
| --- | --- |
| T Conglomerate (Case #1) | Several (Hong Kong, Singapore) |
| D Conglomerate (Case #2) | Global Manager-US |
| ASH Conglomerate (Case #3) | Matrix managers-China/US |
| Genteli Telecom (Case #4) | International Manager-US |
| ABC Printing (Case #5) | International Manager-US |

In these instances, we have 3 varieties of culture, and each needs attention:

- **Home office culture (North America, Europe or Australia)**
    - Home office executives travel through China
    - Sales/marketing account executives handle global accounts with a presence in China
    - Material management/purchasing executives handling global accounts seek suppliers in China
    - Functional experts (engineering, finance, IT, HR) are responsible for identifying, screening, and training functional employees
- **The expatriates' team culture**
    - Expatriates from the home office
    - Expatriates from regional offices
    - Expatriates from Taiwan and Hong Kong
- **The local managers' culture**
    - Local Chinese trained by expat and functional experts

This is now your issue: **Which culture will dominate your China operation?** The home office culture, in a way, is "transferred" to China, but only in pieces since the "home managers" are not on the ground often. Next, your expatriates' team culture is significant, but varies from the source (home, or regional, or Taiwan/Hong Kong office). And employees outnumber the expatriates on the ground. Finally, the local employees you recruit will also impact and influence the local managers' culture.

So, the answer is: It depends. Consider the possibilities.

*The home office culture (North America, Europe or Australia)*

The source of the culture: Road warriors. These are based in your home office and they support the domestic business growth we discussed earlier (*Chapter 1*, and *Exhibit 1-1*, Business Life Cycle [or BLC] Phases 1-3). As your China business starts up and grows through BLC Phases 4 and 5, your road warriors begin to help transfer core competencies to China.

More likely than not, the success factors at "home" are not reproducible in China. So your domestic process that your road warriors know best must be customized–to deliver results in China. It's crucial for your road warriors to share (while traveling in China) their success factors at home.

This is one issue. A second issue: Road warriors cannot customize your process for the China market because you're best equipped to do that.

> **Processes at home and in China are related**, for good or ill. If you have a strong continuous improvement culture at home (e.g., at D Conglomerate, *Case #2*), you have tools to communicate continuous improvement in China. But if you have aggressive accounting at "home," as with the T Conglomerate case (*Case #1*), it's pretty likely that you have aggressive accounting in China–and that's worrisome. And in our ABC Printing example (*Case #5*), effective "home" communications can be neutralized when politics blocks communication channels from China.

Culture is reflected in actions and words, but actions dominate. People need to "walk the talk." A company may have exceptional messages, but it will not establish a **character-centric culture** if its road warriors fail to execute. At ABC Printing (*Case #5*), a 2-year development program looked attractive to Mark Chen, but he never experienced it. This simply reaffirms the idea that strategy without precise execution is strategy wasted. For excellent details on this, see *Execution*, written by Larry Bossidy and Ram Charan in 2002[42].

> One more idea on home office culture: Some issues may annoy you–e.g., cell phones that stay on during meetings. But if laws aren't violated, stay open minded and pause before you act. Practice identifying the fine line between being flexible, and being culturally insensitive. You lose if you presume yours is a superior culture at all times.

Successful cultures like Danaher DBS's work globally, because they have the flexibility needed for local implementation. To paraphrase China's recent leader Deng Xiao-ping: "It does not matter if it is a black cat or a white cat, as long as the cat catches the mouse." It remains to be seen who will build the best mouse trap through character-centric healthy cultures.

## *The expatriates' team culture*[43]

Drawing from our case studies, China operations are managed by expatriates with the following Nationalities:

| | Nationalities of Expatriates from | | |
|---|---|---|---|
| Case Study | Home Office | Regional Office | Taiwan Hong Kong |
| T Conglomerate (*Case #1*) | US | UK, US, AUS | Hong Kong |
| D Conglomerate (*Case #2*) | US | none | Taiwan |
| ASH Conglomerate (*Case #3*) | US | Sing, US | none |
| Genteli Telecom (*Case #4*) | US | none | none |
| ABC Printing (*Case #5*) | US | none | Hong Kong |

For developing the China team's culture, the key question remains: To what extent have your expats been properly motivated (see *Chapters 3-5*)? If expat assignments aren't seen as career development paths for superior employees, the result is higher costs and higher turnover. This could significantly delay and severely impact your ability to deliver competitive advantage for your home office. And it will create "misdirected" cultures where expatriates look out for themselves, but not for their company.

> The T Conglomerate environment (*Case #1*) shows "pyramid culture": Hong Kong expatriates had the support of their Singapore regional office, and targeted short term profit and cash flow—as long as the activities were legal. What was ignored: Minimal training, high employee turnover, scant employee benefits, and Finance operating ineffectively, but focused squarely on reducing taxes. All the activities were legal, but had a cost.

On a broader scale, the easiest place to appreciate the value of your expatriate culture is through functional experts. Your top sales person knows the products or services features and benefits, along with competition very well. Engineers know technical specifications and can manage machinery performance very well. Finance managers know the structure of the subsidiary ledgers that tie to the general ledger and reveal insights about operational performance.

Functional experts must work with teammates in China in order to transfer their skills to the local employees. Since it is nearly impossible to establish the scope of products and services in order to discuss the Sales function and there are intricate trade secrets related topics in engineering, let's use financial reporting as an illustrative example.

To effectively develop a Finance function, for instance, the finance functional expert must have

• Motivated trainees, and

• Effective channels of communication.

Recruiting trainees (for local staff) is a vital issue normally handled by Human Resources. But experienced expatriates are also excellent resources—if personal relationships and relatives are not involved. The result: You can select and retain effective trainees if you use quality training and the functional expert can handle the trainees.

For training, your communication channel can be English or Chinese. In this case, **expatriates who can communicate in Chinese** are critical. The Taiwan and Hong Kong expatriates can be especially effective, particularly if they're familiar with Western management practices, or because they're fluent in either language. If this skill transfer training must be conducted in English only, it takes longer.

We should underscore the goal: Don't simply feed fish to your local employees; teach them how to fish—as the saying goes. Don't describe a financial procedure. Show why it's valuable to your Chinese operations and key financial measures, and show how to test the strength of these measures to help your Chinese operations. Local staffers will find this difficult because the topics aren't taught in Chinese schools. But by doing it this way and you can shift the burden of learning to those who must claim ownership of your procedures.

As a team, expatriates must focus on your profit and growth targets. Constructive, direct feedback helps drives success. Open communications are illustrated in the ABC Printing case (*Case #5*): When one manager becomes obstructionist, an American expatriate trainer points out that the manager's actions significantly complicate another manager's efforts to build a team. (And in the D Conglomerate case [*Case #2*], the open discussion of the Qingdao investment shows the success of Policy Deployment.)

### *The local managers' culture*

Your local managers and employees are mirrors that reflect the culture and character of your expatriates. Immediate features that are visible include English abilities, customer focus, skills acquisition, loyalty, and general business etiquette–in meeting home office visitors or expatriates. Whether the local managers, as a team, make decisions like your home office is a clear indicator of how your expatriates are doing.

In other words, your local managers can give you insights into the character of your expatriates. If you do a 360 degree survey as a performance review (see *Chapter 4*), you will have annual assessments of expatriate performance and build your character-centric culture in China.

A word about "cultural stereotypes": The profile of local managers in China is that they are quiet, and seem to lack initiative. They speak when spoken to, and aren't boastful about their contributions. This does not mean lack of competence. In fact, two factors are usually at play here:

- Tradition-bound behavior
- Ability in handling English conversation

Traditionally, Chinese businesses are run by the most senior manager (the country was ruled by an Emperor), independent of competence. A key to the lack of Western-style progress in

**Note**

Chinese society was the high degree of nepotism. Example: Virtually all emperors passed their throne on only to their oldest son[44]. When you combine this nepotism with the Confucian principle of respect for the elderly, what you have is an introverted "public behavior" visible in every person not in a "chain of command." This is clearly changing, but we will continue to see a transition period.

As for English, local Chinese employees value the opportunities to communicate in English because they lack such opportunities in China. They usually focus first on listening skills to make sure they understand what is being communicated. (It remains difficult to express yourself without some level of comfort with spoken English.) English speakers who try to learn conversational Chinese understand this immediately.

To recap: The critical role of expatriates, in their fiduciary roles especially, is to develop teams that fully understand your character-centric cultural needs. In the next Chapter, we offer key guides for understanding your local Chinese employees.

*The thing always happens that you really believe in;*
*and the belief in a thing makes it happen.*

*—Frank Lloyd Wright*

# CHAPTER 6
# WORKSHEET

1. I have ___1 ___2 ___3 culture(s) in China. Strongest in influence is-

   ____Home Office ____Expatriates ____Local Management

2. I ___advocate ___expect ___ am not concerned whether my employees have:
   a. The "character" to do the "right thing when no one is looking"?
      ___Y ___N
   b. Strong focus on profit, and minimizing cost so long as the company complies with the market and country laws and regulations? ___Y ___N

3. Model companies with strong, healthy cultures for me are:

   _____


4. I communicate culture in the form of:

   _____


5. If I ask my "counterpart community" (my customers, partners and suppliers in China) about my culture, they would say the following:

   _____

Key remaining issues in my company culture and in our character-centric processes:

_____

_____

_____

*As we live, so we learn.*

—*Yiddish Proverb*

# Chapter 7

# Managing your local Chinese employees

## Executive Summary

Note

- **Skill profile for local Chinese employees**: *They're well educated and have varying skills in conversational English. Important: They choose a lifestyle when they join your company and are very willing to learn.*
- **Major motivators for local Chinese employees**: *They want to contribute to society, prefer social groupings at work, and they focus on people, not companies.*
- **Your role**: *Stay open minded, use continuous improvement in your thinking to deal with local business practices–e.g., their attitude to sharing salary information.*

Once your China-based operation is humming, what will drive its success?

Most of it depends on your Chinese managers and workers. Ultimately, the strength of your expatriate team is helpful but not decisive. **What will be decisive is how–once your expatriate team creates your processes–your Chinese workers "take up the baton" and do their part.** Few businesses in China succeed if they lack strong teams of Chinese workers.

Note

How can you staff your China operation to do this well? If you want educated staff, China produces about the same number of engineering and science graduates as the US does–465,000 graduates (in 2001)[45].

To gauge their performance, we can consider their results on standardized tests widely used in the US.

SAT tests are still rare outside the International Schools. But many Chinese high school students take the Test of English as a Foreign Language (TOEFL) or Graduate Record Examinations (GRE for Graduate School Admission). Because TOEFL does not require oral communications, Chinese students generally do well. In fact the 1998-1999 Educational Testing Service ranked Chinese students fourth in TOEFL scores in Asia at 562 points (maximum: 677 points). This is just 22 points below the Asian TOEFL score leader Philippines.[46]

And talented, local Chinese usually have 3 choices in a business career:

- **State Owned Enterprises** (SOEs)–These offer more job security, less workload, and less salary. When the laws for foreign enterprises were initially created, the foreign enterprises would pay a 20% salary premium. In these organizations, their career advancement is based on performance, and on existing relationships.

- **Privately held companies**–These offer great potential, but the Chinese government officially recognized the contribution from these companies in 2001-2, and there is significant variation in the type of opportunities offered.

- **Foreign enterprises**–The "Chinese street" knows these have a reputation for career advancement based on performance (not Pai Ma Pi or "brown-nosing"). In new, growing businesses, the learning experience in an English speaking environment, with the right coach, is very attractive.

When they choose you as the employer, the local Chinese choose a lifestyle. They want and expect career advancement through performance, and the other advantages you offer.

For your expatriates, meanwhile, it's the ability to communicate in English that serves as the bridge to managing Chinese workers. But to understand how that works, and the variations in these skills, let's consider that competency fully.

By current Chinese standards, English skill competencies vary widely among Chinese workers. The following table represents typical skill levels:

| <u>Skill Level</u> | <u>Schooling</u> | <u>Abilities</u> |
| --- | --- | --- |
| Level 4 | College graduates | Read, write (some) |
| Level 5 | Not used | |
| Level 6 | College graduates | Low fluency |
| Level 7 | Not used | |
| Level 8 | English majors | High fluency |
| **Upper Levels** | Varied | Proficient fluency |

College graduates usually have a minimum Level 4 competency. Level 6 represents English fluency, but many still lack oral communications skills because they are not exposed to English regularly. (Recreational parks in China have Saturday and Sunday morning "English Club" gatherings where students practice conversation.) Level 8 is reserved for English majors who are highly fluent English speakers. Higher levels are for interpreters and translators.

Most non-English majors graduate to Level 6 after 4 years of college but there is a significant variation in their conversational abilities.

Traditionally, Chinese educational style calls for a rigid, solitary course of study, with parents feeding nutritious food to the child to increase his or her stamina. (Note: We say "child" because China's official policy since 1981[47] is "one family, one child"–used to slow population growth. This has been relaxed in some cities: Married couples who are both single children are allowed to have two children.)

In this environment, capable students in non-"English major" tracks often lack spoken English competency. If they can communicate fluently in English, they command a substantial salary premium. So they're mobile workers. The best way to retain them is not with salary, but with a healthy culture coupled with a strong commitment to development.

As a result, the coaching skills of your expatriates will shape the culture of local Chinese employees. For recruiting tasks, expats with Chinese language abilities have a substantial advantage and a larger pool of capable local Chinese to work with, and at lower cost.

In light of a Hewitt Associates survey of 13,000 employees in 50 foreign companies in China[37] (polled in 2001), **the top three factors that motivate local Chinese employees** are "purpose," "work-life," and "management." As we've said, we know they like to contribute to society, work in social teams, and prefer focusing on people, not companies.

> **If you want to attract capable Chinese employees, the next 5 years represent a watershed.** China is at a critical juncture in its management development. As many of the pre-Cultural Revolution-Era managers retire, many less-educated Cultural Revolution cadres will rely on the post-Cultural Revolution ("pCR") educated managers. Many of these newer "pCR"-educated managers now do work that their supervisors are responsible for. If language is not a barrier, you can recruit these "pCR" managers today. *If you wait*, you will have a tougher time recruiting capable local managers because they will already be managing Chinese businesses.

As expatriates recruit and develop local talent, your best bet is to maintain continuity for the time when your expatriates will repatriate. The key skill you want them to have is coaching and mentoring capabilities. So throughout your communications, stress your successful repatriations, and remind everyone–expats returning and local Chinese continuing in China–about **the all-important "coaching support"** you offer local Chinese staffers. This is a healthy culture practice, and sustains profitable growth.

Also be aware that there are few personal secrets in China. Evidence: People share salary information readily. While these attitudes are changing, Chinese still hand out manually produced "tally strips," detailing every single item of pay. Example: Local currency bonus payments of 2 Renmenbi (or RMB, the local currency) are paid monthly to married workers with one child. Every item on this strip was known, and shared among the workers. The range of salary between the senior manager and the entry level clerk was narrow. It is common to ask "what's your salary?" Most Chinese openly share salary information.

**Chinese prefer sharing salary information**–regardless of its consequences–because they're curious about the value of different types of work (e.g., the title of "senior engineer" commands premium pay). In effect, this is the Chinese version of "pay for performance" where they try to seek jobs that pay well.

In this environment, you'll find it tough to justify why chauffeurs for your expatriates might command higher salaries than senior engineers in the same operation. To manage this issue, you need a transitional execution strategy. Example: Enact and distribute a written policy that "sharing of compensation information violates company policy, and is subject to severe penalties (including termination)." The benefit: This arms your expats with tactics for responding to their inquisitive Chinese staffers, and helps them keep similar confidences in social gatherings.

As growing numbers of local managers receive higher performance-based salaries, **reinforce the confidentiality of a salary information policy**. The termination clause is normally a sufficient deterrent, but be prepared to enforce the policy if blatant violators persist. Over time, higher-paid Chinese managers will learn to keep this information confidential, and the culture will benefit along with this new habit of thinking.

> Since you'll have pay differentials between local Chinese and expatriates, let's briefly **consider the concept of equal pay for equal work**. Take compensation in Research & Development department as your departure point. Your must target these assets:

- *Access to knowledge*
  - Trade secrets–note that patents are already public documents
  - Information searches that people use
  - Your key process map from concept to market (which often requires a team)
- *Tools*
  - Operating high value precision equipment
  - Design/layout experiments that test hypotheses
  - Experimental design to organize raw data and extract analytical information
- *Teamwork*
  - Fellow scientists, engineers
  - Technicians, MSDS data analysts
  - Others helping move ideas from "concept to customer"
- *Quality*
  - Government test procedures, approvals
  - Certification requirements
  - Customer acceptance and liability insurance
- *Value creation*
  - Consumer prices in Chinese are generally lower or much lower than prices in US, Europe and Australia. Prices for industrial products and services vary significantly according to supply and demand.
  - Chinese costs are highly varied and difficult to manage. For low-cost-labor products and services, business costs such as expatriates, training, translation, marketing/sales/distribution costs, Value Added Tax, and other taxation add significant burdens to the overall cost of business.

How do you create a solution everyone can live with when it comes to salary? With a continuous improvement environment at your home office, you should be further along on the learning curve (more cumulative experience and more mature processes) than your Chinese operation. Use that information to

- Have your Chinese employees understand the value of the learning curve and continuous improvement
- Use your own processes to help your Chinese operation push to continually improve
- Identify, at home and abroad (in China), the resources your Chinese managers need to improve
- Allocate resources and salary to support growth in both the home office and your Chinese operation.

**Target the continuous improvement process, not personalities**, and you can leverage this sensitive transition in China. You'll take an unstable operation, and convert it into a healthy culture. This is the win-win, and the broad-base solution everyone can live with.

The success of your local Chinese staff depends on its selection, and its "constant coaches," your expats. If the expatriates are managed well, and manage others well, your local Chinese employees will succeed.

**Remember: Your local Chinese employees are the ones who ultimately guarantee the delivery of profit in China.**

*I have found the best way to give advice to your children is,
first find out what they want. Then advise them to do it.*

*—Harry S Truman (1884-1972)*

# CHAPTER 7
# WORKSHEET

1.  The three most important reasons why local Chinese join my company are:

    a. _____

    b. _____

    c. _____

2.  I think my local Chinese employees can conduct business meetings in English-

    _____ Fluently　　　_____ Adequately　　　_____ Poorly

    My solution for this is to: _____

3.  I have ways to deal with sensitive local business practices by employees:

    | Local Business Practice | My Company Policy |
    | --- | --- |
    | #1 Sharing of Salary Information | _____ |
    | #2_____ | _____ |
    | #3_____ | _____ |

4.  I have several effective ways of recruiting/developing local Chinese employees:

    _____

    _____

    _____

5. My local Chinese employees understand my company culture

   ___ Well   ___Moderately   ___Inadequately

Key issues I see in my local Chinese workforce:

_____

_____

*Don't judge a man by the words of his mother,*
*listen to the comments of his neighbours.*

*—Yiddish Proverb*

## Chapter 8

# Taiwan and Hong Kong roles in Greater China business

<u>Note</u>            *Executive Summary*

- Taiwanese expatriates fit a profile: *Entrepreneurially-minded operations managers focused strongly on traditional management techniques, less on management processes.*

- Hong Kong expatriates represent other skill sets: *They often are strong in architecture, finance and distribution skills.*

- Culturally-based practices can interfere with each other: *Monitor the culture being introduced by Taiwanese or Hong Kong expats. Ensure their focus accelerates growth in China-without divergent from your "home office" practices.*

**Will your office suffer from a "war of cultures"?**

Focus, for a moment, on your Taiwan and Hong Kong employees, and right away, you'll see they bring different cultural practices "to the table" as they help you grow in Greater China. It's just a question of how you manage them. (Note: Macau managers ready to work with foreign companies usually migrate to

116

Hong Kong.) Most of your sourcing of managers from points beyond China will be from Hong Kong and Taiwan.

So how do you handle the "other" China expats? First of all, the idea of completing an expatriate assignment quickly does not work with Taiwanese and Hong Kong expats, because your "home office" is not their home. Instead, you must consider career development headed towards a regional role or functional expertise. That may be more workable.

**SNAPSHOT**: The Mosaic that is Greater China Today

Greater China consists of China, Taiwan, Hong Kong, and Macau. In this extended region, 1.3 billion people are in China, 23 million in Taiwan, 6 million in Hong Kong, and 0.4 million in Macau. Taiwan and Hong Kong have been 2 of the so-called Asian "Tigers" for two decades now.

*China*

As for Chinese demographics, youth dominates and grew from 540 million in 1949 to 1.3 billion today (140% growth in 53 years).[48]

This is remarkable if you simply review the population growth from 1600 to 1949:

| Year: | 1600 | 1850 | 1949 | 2003 |
|---|---|---|---|---|
| Population: (Millions) | 200 | 450 | 540 | 1300 |

It took 350 years to increase the population by 340 million. **In just 53 years, China spiked its population by 760 million**.

*Macau*

Macau was the first Far Eastern European settlement in the 16th century, and colonized by Portuguese. Macau was returned to China on December 20, 1999. It is well known as a gambling enclave.

Note

### Taiwan

Taiwan was an early European settlement in the Far East in the 16th century, occupied first by Portuguese, then the Dutch. China's Cheng Cheng-kung (or Koxinga) arrived to defeat the Dutch in 1662 and occupy Taiwan.

Since that point, the one major historical date important for this brief historical tour is the 1894-1895 period, when the Sino-Japanese War was triggered by a dispute over control of Korea.

To end the Sino-Japanese War in 1895, China ceded Taiwan to Japan by signing the Treaty of Shimonoseki. Japan then occupied Taiwan until 1945 when China reacquired it. Nationalist Chinese government was established in Taiwan in 1949.

Since 1949, China has considered Taiwan a renegade province. As of 2003, direct travel between Taiwan and China remains forbidden. There is less restriction of investment, since the Taiwanese have invested over US$70 billion[45] in China.

### Hong Kong

Hong Kong consists of Hong Kong Island, Kowloon, the New Territories and some surrounding islands in the Pearl River delta. Hong Kong Island was ceded to Britain in 1842 during the Opium War. Kowloon and New Territories were leased for 99 years in 1898. In 1997, Britain returned the entire British Crown Colony, including Hong Kong Island, back to China.

Economically, Hong Kong is the "free port" Milton Friedman sees as the success story-model free enterprise[49]. With an advanced finance and logistics infrastructure and a Westernized economy, it's a portal for entry into China (since 1978), and continues to play an important role today.

While Greater China is definitely Chinese, you do see remnants of foreign influence: Japanese influence in Taiwan, British influence in Hong Kong, and Portuguese influence in Macau.

**Given this picture, where do Taiwan and Hong Kong expatriates fit in your organization?** Consider, first, the many languages they use.

The written language of Taiwan and Hong Kong is "traditional Chinese," while China uses "simplified Chinese" for its 1.3 billion. (Singapore is seen as culturally closer to China since Singapore has adopted "simplified Chinese" as its official written language.) Because simplified Chinese is about 50 years old, many Greater Chinese still read traditional and simplified writings. However, China does not sanction traditional Chinese. Chinese familiar only with simplified Chinese can only guess at the traditional Chinese literature in Taiwan and Hong Kong.

Meanwhile, Taiwan's official spoken language is Mandarin, as in China. There are local Taiwanese dialect deriving from China's Fujian province (across the Strait from Taiwan). But few Mandarin speakers understand the local Taiwanese dialect. In Hong Kong, the "lingua franca" is Cantonese, and the population cannot communicate in Mandarin. But most managers learn to communicate in Mandarin, and are quite fluent.

*Taiwan expatriates*

Taiwanese expatriates are excellent managers, but introduce an additional culture strand more congruent with Chinese entrepreneurs than multinational corporations. And Taiwanese entrepreneurial managers tend to use more autocratic decision making, not team and consensus building. This will confuse your Chinese workers if you're moving toward a strong team focus.

**RECOMMENDATION: Be extra vigilant** about this at "startup time" since processes are poorly defined under startup conditions. And first impressions may work against you if you launch with significant "signals" and processes established by an autocratic style of management.

Your Taiwanese expatriates must understand and commit to managing your processes. The key to sustained profitable growth: **Ensure you train these Taiwan expatriates to foster a continuous improvement culture.** That happen successfully mainly with "team environments."

In turn, you will motivate Taiwanese managers by explaining the benefits of new job security, new career development paths and improved team morale for doing the hard work required by startup operations.

With over US$70 billion Taiwanese investment, you may be able to leverage your Taiwanese operation to increase your business opportunities in China. In T Conglomerate (*Case #1*), Mark Chen organized the Taiwanese team to train with the Chinese team to pursue Taiwanese invested Fire and Security projects in China. In D Conglomerate (*Case #2*), several Taiwanese companies with extensive China operations were acquired to jump start the tools business in China.

### Hong Kong expatriates

Your Hong Kong expatriates generally reflect the strengths of Hong Kong. Consider how these strengths have evolved over time.

#### The strengths of Hong Kong

**For decades, Hong Kong has been a smaller metropolis thriving on finance and trade into and out of China.** The island culture is living proof of the adage about how and where to "site" your business: "It's all a matter of location, location, location." Some of earth's wealthiest are Hong Kong residents (e.g., Li Kai-Shing). Many became wealthy through real estate investments.

Because of the bursting of financial and tech bubbles since 2000, real estate values have declined somewhat. After all, any company can trade with China without using Hong Kong as the "middleman." Many Hong Kong residents are caught up in this transition, and face negative home equity in their residences.

Normally, when real estate is high-priced, cities move to "compact" their business zones. But Hong Kong's climate works against that somewhat: As in Los Angeles, there are mudslides, lightning and some earthquakes.

So, architectural engineering has stepped forward, and flourished. Hong Kong now boasts one of the precious skylines on earth. And 2 of the top 10 tallest buildings in the world are in Hong Kong.

And to support high volume trade, cities need strong financial infrastructures, to better respond to global companies. Hong Kong now has a strong reputation as a regional financial center.

Hong Kong is also one of the busiest ports (as is Singapore) in container volume. To manage this volume, Hong Kong is building strong information technology (IT) infrastructure to upgrade its reach in logistics and distribution. Fiber optic cable and wireless broadband are also widely available and they now connect Hong Kong to the rest of the world.

To recap Hong Kong's key strengths:

- Architectural engineering
- Finance
- Logistics and distribution

If you need managers from these areas, Hong Kong expats can be strong teammates. But they tend to be weaker coaches (for a variety of reasons). As most people living in, or close to developing countries, they are strong workers with highly refined survival skills. Just as with Taiwanese, your key to profitable growth is to ensure you train Hong Kong expats to maintain a continuous improvement culture.

### Managing Taiwan and Hong Kong expatriates

As we've suggested earlier, the twin roles of Taiwan and Hong Kong in your Greater China business ventures depend on the strength of your home office processes and team.

**You must be able to identify, and extend your home office culture and processes** into your China-based operation. This is a sizeable task.

**If you have strong "home" teams to build China operations,** you may choose to source expats from areas other than Taiwan and Hong Kong. Instead, you can use home office expatriates to train your local Chinese.

As a result, you'll gain a simple but distinct advantage: In your China-based startup, you will launch using well-tested processes, and begin growing your business with a sharpened focus. A well-defined simply-focused culture helps you target growth and delivers results faster.

On the other hand, if you take on Taiwan and Hong Kong expats, you must communicate your culture and expectations clearly. If you forego these earlier opportunities, you may lose a lot of ground. If you fail to manage these expats properly, you're exactly like a banker financing an unproven operational team (as we see in T Conglomerate–*Case #1*).

Instead, carefully shortlist the benefits of Taiwan and Hong Kong expatriates, and use simple cost-benefit analysis. While they clearly can contribute, they may also add new cultural strands that "complect" your China-based operation. But you want simplicity, not complexity.

In short, Taiwanese and Hong Kong expatriates will support you if their job security remains affirmed (not threatened). So long as they understand the sensitivity of startup operations, and respect and uphold your values, and above all, as long as they execute, they can be among your best managers.

When appropriately motivated and managed, they can become local assets that sustain your competitive advantage as you build out your business.

**As you look long-term at your sourcing needs, you may need to enrich your toolkit for motivating and managing Taiwan and Hong Kong expatriates**. This is a more complex topic than we're prepared to address in these pages.

This much is certain: As you expand beyond a regional role, and use multi-cultural teams for your Greater China market, you may well benefit from the advice of organizational development consultants.

*A faithful friend is a strong defense: and*
*he that hath found such an one hath found a treasure.*

*—Ecclesiasticus, 6:14*

# CHAPTER 8
# WORKSHEET

1.  I have ___ Hong Kong plus ___ Taiwan expats in my China team responsible for…

    _____

    _____

    For them, I spend US$_____ annually on salaries and development.

2.  We discussed their roles in our China-based operation on _____

    Their biggest concern was _____

    I plan to address this by _____

3.  Future plans for them call for _____

4.  Key feedback on our Hong Kong/Taiwanese expats, from local Chinese employees: _____

    _____

    We plan to respond to this with the following steps:

    _____

5.  We communicate with our Hong Kong and Taiwan expats in these ways:

    a.  Email ____%

    b.  Meeting ____%

    c.  Telephone ____%

d. Other ____% (Specify: _____)

    Total      100 %

Key issues I see in my Taiwan and Hong Kong expatriate workforce:

_____

_____

*Opportunities are usually disguised as hard work,*
*so most people don't recognize them.*

*—Ann Landers*

# Section IV

# Summary and Workbook

You've reviewed these ideas in our earlier chapters:

- China's promise as a market full of attractive, profitable opportunities is very real, but its high-stakes business challenges are equally real.

- *"People are your most valuable assets and expatriates are your change agents"*–an idea stressed by French expatriate Z. Zhang, President of North Asia, Sidel, and formerly Vice President, Schneider Electric China.

- Healthy cultures and strong "character-centric" set of practices will establish and sustain your profitable growth.

It's time to collect and "aggregate" these ideas in a single segment. We begin by illustrating these ideas, to better prepare you for your China operations in the Workbook in Chapter 10.

The process of building any China operation requires a solid foundation from your home office. The more solid, the better documented your home office processes, the higher is your likelihood of success in China.

While creating short term profit is possible without a solid home office foundation, you will face hurdles in trying to sustain it over time.

**This is one of the core ideas in this book: You must plan for a sustainable, profitable growth path.** There is no perfection, no magic in any continuous process. All processes have strengths and weaknesses, and all you can do is undertake to improve them.

**The rate of your profitability growth will be governed by the weakest links in your process skills.** Typically, the weakest link today is managing your expatriates' expectations–which directly impact your speed of localization.

**To shift from reading into action, we urge you to use our** *"30 Minute Workbook"*–designed and created to help you identify and evaluate the weakest points in your processes.

**Do that, and you'll have a solid, success path to new profits and a growing business in Greater China.**

*It's the action, not the fruit of the action,*
*that's important. You have to do the right thing.*
*It may not be in your power, may not be in your time,*
*that there'll be any fruit.*
*But that doesn't mean you stop doing the right thing.*
*You may never know what results come from your action.*
*But if you do nothing, there will be no result.*

—*Gandhi*

# Chapter 9

# Summary

## *Executive Summary*

<u>Note</u>

- *While China is a lucrative market,* **your efforts in China are only as strong as the weakest link**–*your ability to marshal the resources your expatriates need to succeed.*

- **Your most important step now is to successfully repatriate** *your expatriates upon completion of their assignments which will attract strong candidates for future overseas assignments.*

- **Put overseas assignments on the critical path to successful careers** *in your company and create a continuous improvement environment for a global healthy culture that is locally managed.*

---

Of 42 million business enterprises[6] in the US, Europe, and Australia, your company is among the elite group exploring and investing US$40-70 billion annually in foreign direct investment in China[7]. You also help funnel US$30-50 billion in expatriate expenses[21] to manage 25,000 non-Chinese funded enterprises with US$300 billion sales in 2000 after growing over 19% from 1999.

**You probably expect at least double digit compounded annual growth rates** (CAGR)–and you have reason to do so. If you're contributing to the companies averaging US$12 million in annual sales (2000), you're part of a bevy of small enterprises with a **high growth vision**. You might even be negotiating with some of the 165,000 Chinese enterprises right now as part of the US$500 billion in import and export trading being trans-acted in China[50]. Exhibit 9-1 sums up all of this for you.

There is pressure for you to raise your growth rate as China operates now under WTO rules, having joined in 2001. You might have expectations for being cited among the best compa-nies in China.

Based on available data and much longer histories elsewhere, we can say that the best US companies achieve 24-32% higher return than other companies over 3, 5 and 10-year measurement timelines[40]. Inject this level of improvement into your potential China operations, and you can save over US$1 billion in expa-triate expenses alone each and every year.

**So where is the "low-hanging fruit" for performance improve-ment in China for you?** How can you begin emulating these impressive returns found among elite US companies?

Given our strategic case studies and extensive anecdotal evi-dence, your **weakest "mission critical" area and your root cause of failure, revolve around the management of expectations with expatriates**, especially during repatriation. Despite spend-ing US$30-50 billion annually on 150,000 expatriates as com-panies enter the China market, US, European and Australian companies simply fail–that's the right word, "fail"–to optimize their employees high potential. **By strengthening "mission-crit-ical" areas**, you can expect superior business performance.

You must simply select your expatriates wisely, and motivate them to develop local managers (once both are "on the

**Exhibit 9-1**
**Summary Flow Chart**

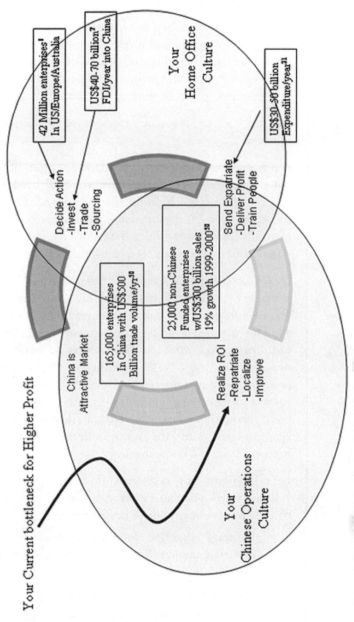

42 Million enterprises[1]
In US/Europe/Australia

US$40-70 billion[7]
FDI/year into China

US$30-50 billion
Expenditure/year[21]

Your
Home Office
Culture

Decide Action
-Invest
-Trade
-Sourcing

Send Expatriate
-Deliver Profit
-Train People

China is
Attractive Market

165,000 enterprises
In China with US$500
Billion trade volume/yr[55]

25,000 non-Chinese
Funded enterprises
w/US$300 billion sales
19% growth 1999-2000[58]

Realize ROI
-Repatriate
-Localize
-Improve

Your Current bottleneck for Higher Profit

Your
Chinese Operations
Culture

Source: Based on 2000-2001 data. See footnotes for details.

ground"), and **you will have a team well-matched to address your "mission-critical" areas.**

The key areas, according to George Chu, Chief Consultant for Zhong Zi Company and former Vice President of Coca Cola China, are "speed, quality, and process of localization." Mitigate those weak points, and in turn, this puts you on a continuous improvement road that remains continuous.

**You can succeed,** if you want to succeed–that's the message of this book.

Is it enough to target recruitment and retention of high-potential expatriates? Well, for starters, you will need to motivate them to optimize their productivity. As the ASH Conglomerate situation (*Case #3*) demonstrates, you can accelerate the growth of your successful startup, and enhance the chances for scaling your business operations, and sustain higher rates of growth.

One success factor is having an expatriate like Mark Chen, a manager flying some 80 hours monthly (for over a year) to bring resources together for China-based operations. And that was not all: This required a strong commitment to expand the operations from a successful base. The impressive results: The operation delivered over 30% operating profit margin, the only positive profit margin reported by ASH Conglomerate for 5 years in its China operations. In that case, a foundation was laid, but a partnership relationship failed to develop because of management changes and the lack of "refreshed" management commitment from the home team.

**Let's highlight our takeaways from our twin models**, the Business Life Cycle and Career Life Cycle. Your operations will succeed by focusing on these key elements:

- **Leverage superior products and services from the domestic market** (Phases 1-3 of Business Life Cycle)
  - Know what you offer, and how it represents competitive advantage versus your rivals
  - Use clear messages about strength, and listen for how that strength fits in customers' requirements in China

- **Motivate expatriates to carry your sustainable competitive advantages overseas quickly.** Support them from the home office with strong functional team leaders and strong character-centric focus (Business Life Cycle–Phase 4)

  - Understand the requirements for motivating expatriates (Career Life Cycle)

  - Listen and respond to the resource issues, and prioritize them for continuous improvement

  - Recognize the key value of expats' families and children.

- **Localize and empower local employees** (Phase 5a of Business Life Cycle)

  - Reinforce professional development plans with empathy, and monitor the development of local talent so it's consistent with home office culture

  - Differentiate competent employees from those whose main strength is the ability to communicate in English

  - Develop newly-hired local Chinese employees with purpose and balanced work-life

  - Establish policies to develop and retain Taiwan and Hong Kong expatriates

- **Repatriate or expand expatriate responsibilities progressively** (Business Life Cycle Phase 5b)

  - Consider having expats keep some responsibility after repatriation

  - Do NOT violate the trust the expats place on the company

  - Trust building and keeping-this can be the weakest point among the US's US$30-50 billion/year investment

- **Establish continuity and stay vigilant for continuous improvement-and healthy cultural practices.** Identify the character-centric practices that sustain growth. (Business Life Cycle-Phase 6)

  - What should you reinforce in your resources or your documentation?

- Anticipate: Where might your next major weak spot surface as your business grows, and how can you address it?

In addition, we have the lessons of the Business Life Cycle Phases.

*Leverage superior products and services from your domestic market-Business Life Cycle Phases 1-3*

**Your domestic success**–in the US market, if you represent a US company–**establishes foundations for overseas success**. For conglomerates, the value in diverse products and services is to prioritize the attractive opportunities, so you can better pursue them according to targeted customer requirements. Processes such as the Danaher Business System (*Exhibit 2-1*) are excellent tools applicable worldwide. The stronger the process, in place domestically, the faster the profitable growth possible overseas. Mark Chen, for instance, in ASH Conglomerate (*Case #3*) illustrated the strength of the Chinese when they focus on the results.

**Time is the additional dimension here**. The early-adopter China investors have been rewarded with majority ownerships of joint ventures in the country, witness both ASH Conglomerate (*Case #3*) and ABC Printing (*Case #5*). The real market barrier to entry: Majority-owned JVs cannot be duplicated until 2005. But this is also a two edged sword, since there are many opportunities to lose money if you mismanage your steps.

*Motivate expatriates to carry your sustainable competitive advantages overseas quickly-Business Life Cycle Phase 4*

From all available evidence, your expatriates are best treated as transition executives whose mission is to carry your competitive advantage to China, and develop and coach local teams to extend your success into Chinese markets. Their functions are multi-faceted, requiring business, diplomatic, and coaching skills. To sustain profitable growth over time, you must "carry over" a healthy company culture. Consider our examples:

In the situation faced by Genteli Telecom (*Case #4*), the Hong Kong operations were unsustainable because the home team had failed to create a healthy company culture–specifically, a solid financial foundation.

US-based Anheuser-Busch, on the other hand, has been among the "Best Employers in America" (1994)[51] because of its culture. Anheuser-Busch Asia Inc. was one of the top 10 employers in China in 2001. It took 7 years to "translate" its healthy culture into China. Through that painstaking effort, the China-based company might be able to sustain its superior culture as the parent company continues to evolve on its own.

Meanwhile, in terms of developing better processes, D Conglomerate (as we see in *Case #2*) has a Policy Deployment structure to prioritize business decision making. This helps assure the success of its culture, and it's reflected in Wall Street Analysts' premium valuation of the company.

Overseas assignments in general and China assignments especially are excellent opportunities for your top managers. Your superior employees (Career Life Cycle Phase 2 and 3), after all, can now demonstrate their abilities and help deliver performance.

To succeed, they must be culturally sensitive, and develop an inclusive workforce. Does this sound familiar? It's actually a demonstration that your business performance is tied to the value you place on diversity. **Successful expatriates can be most valuable by building a diverse and inclusive workforce in your home office.**

If the overseas assignments are not viewed as part of an attractive career development path, your superior employees will not be attracted to overseas assignments. The chances of success decrease or there may be delays which reduce profit, and increase the difficulties to attract talent for overseas assignments. A vicious cycle emerges.

**Note**

Once your **overseas assignments are put on the critical paths for successful careers, your top employees will compete** for them. Once you follow through with commensurate assignments upon repatriation after successful overseas assignments, even more employees will compete for these China assignments. The employees using business, diplomatic and coaching skills can work together to reduce the length of expatriate assignments. Do that and propitious cycles emerge–all steps are winners.

With Taiwan and Hong Kong expats, they can be effective short term performers by contributing their strengths to manage your China operation. But they must also be coached to drive your home office practices, or another impractical and confused culture will emerge.

As we saw in the T Conglomerate environment (*Case #1*), there were "disconnects" (as US business people say) among (a) the China operations' view, and (b) the Hong Kong office's interpretation of (c) the Singapore office's interpretation of (d) the US business unit's interpretation of (e) the corporate headquarters' interpretation of key policies and procedures.

Solution: The full organization needs an organizational effectiveness assessment to find the optimal way for organizing for China-based profits. It wasn't easy–in fact, it was complex.

*Localize and empower local employees-Business Life Cycle Phase 5a*

**Local managers should expect, and receive coaching from expatriates,** and they must also have business skills along with diplomatic skills. They must communicate the local customs and modify the imported products' (or services') features in ways that deliver higher growth. Motivated by Western management techniques that address work-life balance issues, local managers must understand their role, and not follow procedures mechanically. To stress this one more time: **They must learn "how to fish, not to be fed fish."**

At the same time, you must monitor and manage the influence of Taiwanese and Hong Kong expatriates. Their orientation has a different cultural "weighting," and you should not jeopardize the effectiveness of your China-based operation by mismanaging these other contributions.

**Warning signals**: At times, some expatriate managers will block channels of communication. By the same token, the home office expatriates should prevent that. And communications are key to maintaining continuity, so this is a primary concern.

The best way to effectively maintain open communication channels is through open dialogue with your "**business counterpart community**" of customers, suppliers, partners and employees.

### *Repatriate or expand responsibilities progressively-Business Life Cycle Phase 5b*

All evidence suggests that the primary weak area in expatriate assignments is in repatriation. Without successful repatriation examples, your overseas assignments will take longer and cost more.

To remedy high turnover, you may be opting to hire expatriates already in China. This is a short term solution unless you provide strong support for training these expatriates.

If expatriate assignments are flawed from the start, the image can not be attractive, and top performing managers at home will see that. The impact: It limits the opportunities at the "home" office. Effective repatriation becomes more difficult. A vicious cycle emerges.

But consider the opposite situation. Assume expat assignments are linked to successful repatriation, and assume further that motivated expatriates deliver faster profitable growth. Overseas business expands and more opportunities become available upon repatriation. Remember, successful expatriates have also demonstrated they are strong managers of diverse and inclusive workforces. If they're on critical paths to successful careers, their opportunities should not be limited to overseas assignments. This is the beginning of a propitious cycle.

As you well know, businesses always need balancing acts. If you think about it, there is a similarly fine balance needed in your home office to handle culturally diverse managers and work-forces.

In short, successful expatriates sustain diversity values and focus on business performance. If culturally sensitive managers can drive an inclusive workforce to deliver results in China, think about what they can do to leverage diversity and help you deliver performance in the US.

*Establish continuity and remain vigilant for continuous improvement in a healthy company culture–Business Life Cycle-Phase 6*

There is no substitute for continuous improvement. Arrogance, more than anything else, brings down great empires. China, internally focused for over 5,000 years, has recently awakened to realize the value of joining the global community, and setting aside its inward-focused culture of the past. Western societies cannot afford to become arrogant and lose their global leader-ship position after leading the world through industrialization. The "21st century may belong to Asia," but it needs to be an Asian Pacific century with full participation from the US, Europe and Australia. There are handsome rewards for compa-nies and expatriates: Global culture, locally managed, wins busi-ness wherever it's tried.

**This concludes your "orientation" to profits in China.** Now, you must execute. The ingredients: Substantial commitment, wise choices, and the drive to satisfy new customers on foreign soil. **Are you ready?** Read on.

*How many a man has dated a new era in his life*
*from the reading of a book.*

—Henry David Thoreau

# CHAPTER 9
# WORKSHEET

1. The 3 biggest problems I face in China are:

   a. _____

   b. _____

   c. _____

2. My "scouting report" and business intelligence suggests these are **my hurdles**:

   Product barriers _____

   Purchasing barriers _____

   Governmental barriers _____

   Competitor barriers _____

3. The most important strategic case studies for my operations in China:

   Case Study #_____ Title: _____

   Case Study #_____ Title: _____

4. These strategic cases studies suggest these are the keys for companies like mine:

   _____

   _____

5. My key takeaways from this book are_____

   _____

My next steps in China:

_____

_____

*The doer alone learneth.*

*—Friedrich Nietzsche*

## Chapter 10

# Your "30 Minute Workbook" to build China ventures

Note

*Let's start with an ACTION PLAN, and move into action.*

For starters, assemble your team, and start your team planning for your China business by completing this Workbook.

Do this so you have a clearer picture of how to focus your future China ventures. To help you complete this Workbook, **we collect below** the **executive summaries** and **worksheets** of all chapters shown earlier–to ease the process of reviewing and recapping what you've learned in individual chapters. In addition, the *Chapter 10* Worksheet is a Summary Worksheet unique to this chapter. It sums up your worksheets and helps you focus on your key ideas and operations areas with greatest impact.

**Grab a pen and be ready to begin, right after these next pages.**

The core of this systematic, step-by-step approach: With this "30 Minute Workbook" to build your China ventures, you learn the process of building a successful culture in China operations, along with tools to identify the weakest point in your operations performance. Every process has weaknesses and strengths. By focusing on your weaker areas, you improve the entire process–until you find "quality hurdles" based on the evolution of your business. That is the core of continuous improvement.

Here's your **WHY, WHAT and HOW** blueprint for success.

**Note**

## *WHY DO THIS?*

You've probably heard a great deal in business circles about what it takes to set up China ventures–some of it true, and some perhaps not. If you're looking to succeed with your own China venture, you must know what's effective and what simply will not work. This chapter is based on discussions with many veteran managers who have been executives of multinational corporate operations in China during 1993 and 2003. As a group, these veteran managers have several hundred years' successful China-based experience.

Unlike many other tactics-filled approaches to China that actually are generic "starting foreign ventures" guides, this chapter is a comprehensive, easily customized, and most important, practical approach to your very own China venture's day-to-day challenges.

## *WHAT YOU WILL LEARN*

- *Setting your strategy*
  - How to narrow your focus, succeed, and stand out from the many competitors clamoring to be your neighbors in China.
    - Establishing the "right thinking"
    - Creating your plan
    - Picking your team
- *Motivating your team to implement strategy*
  - How to leverage your planning to meet your revenue goals faster, and at lower cost.
    - Establishing your dominant "people needs" in China
    - Combining incentive compensation and work-life balance issues to build successful cycles
    - Developing attractive repatriation plans so expatriates look forward to their return
      - How to complete their assignments
      - How they can develop local Chinese managers

• *Establishing and keeping the right company culture to succeed*

- Breakthrough operations management—how to create and communicate your operational plans and messages so that they let you break through the marketplace "noise and clutter."

## HOW YOU CAN DO THIS BEST

We use case studies to enrich and sharpen your know-how:

- *Case Study 1*: **Do you foresee facing the problems of creating complex organizations focused on short term income** and cash flow performance? If so, this case study takes you through the experience of local managers who deliver what's expected of them, and offer you insights for assessing your organization.

- *Case Study 2*: **What do you do when you have the right process in place, but the home team responsible for China is unsupportive?** While Wall Street analysts gave this company premium stock evaluations, this case study shows the impact of the failing health of an executive responsible for China, and lack of diversity at the home office.

- *Case Study 3*: **Can you picture the results a Chinese work team can create when it's focused on delivering results?** This case study tells you how a local Chinese workforce can deliver higher productivity than a US workforce within six months of startup—and capture the full value of low cost labor (assuming appropriate training).

- *Case Study 4*: **What happens if the home office lacks the right foundation for starting up overseas?** This case study highlights the perils of being an expatriate whose home office fails financially and runs out of supplemental investments funds.

- *Case Study 5*: **If a senior executive wants to become an expatriate manager, you need systems and processes to screen that employee effectively**—and ensure she or he is the best candidate. This case study shows how an operation that turns profitable after many years can suffer a quick reversal of fortune when the home team lags in understand the ground truth about its China-based operations.

*Before anything else, preparation is the key to success.*

*—Alexander Graham Bell*

# Chapter 1

# Establishing our framework

## Executive Summary

- *China's **market potential is enormous** and your business can benefit from **recently lowered risks** of setting up in China as China begins to conform to WTO's international trade rules*

- *Expatriates drive overseas growth, but the aggregate cost is US$30-50 billion annually. As you will soon see, your mastery of **Phases 4-6 of the "Business Life Cycle"** give you a framework for actively **accelerating your business growth** in China.*

- *As you prepare to deploy your expatriates, you will discover—by "polling" their ideas—that **they succeed to the degree they are successful managers of diverse teams** in the US.*

*It is better to light a candle than to complain about the darkness.*

—R. Herzog

# CHAPTER 1
# WORKSHEET

1.  My market potential in China is: _____ in
    _____industry(ies)

    I am now in Phase (check one): ___Four ___Five ___Six of the Business Life
    Cycle.

2.  We project sales of _____ within _____ years and my reasonable
    profit as a percent of sales is _____%.

    This is based on:
    ___External Consultants ___ Internal Teams ___ Other _____

3. The following are my 3 key assumptions in the China market:

[Example: One standard assumption covers the economic conditions you presume to be operating in China.]

| Assumption | Date of last update | Source |
|---|---|---|
| a. _____ | _____ | _____ |
| b. _____ | _____ | _____ |
| c. _____ | _____ | _____ |

4.  My investment in equipment and facilities is US$_____ which can
    be used over _____ years. My reasonable return as a percent of this invest-
    ment is _____%.

    At the moment-

    ___ I am close to ___ I am not close to achieving that return today, but may
    in ___ years.

5. I have ___ ventures operating now, all averaging _____annual sales

My Key Issues in China:

_____

_____

_____

## Chapter 2

# Understand your goals in China

## *Executive Summary*

- *KEY: **What is your goal in China?** Remember: Skills for lining up suppliers are different from those used to attract customers.*

- *Your critical **success path requires tools** to prioritize your resources and differentiate your business. These tools must also help you communicate and tackle continuous improvement.*

- *For **some helpful examples**, we'll glance at snapshots of Coca Cola, Pepsi, Honeywell, R. R. Donnelley, and McDonald's.*

*Be who you are and say what you feel, because
those who mind don't matter and those who matter don't mind.*

—*Dr. Seuss*

# CHAPTER 2
# WORKSHEET

1. My target in China is to find:
   a. Local suppliers _____
   b. Trading partners _____
   c. Joint venture partners _____
   d. Technologies _____
   e. Local employees _____
   f. Consultants _____
   g. Customers _____

2. The process I have in place is called _____
   This is strong in _____
   And weak in _____

3. My process that I plan to use focuses on:
   a. Financial information _____
   b. Customer information _____
   c. Market/competitor information _____
   d. Production quality _____
   e. Resource allocation _____
   f. Distribution _____

4. The companies I am most interested in China are: _____

_____

5. The information most useful to me in China includes: _____

_____

Key issues I see in my products/services features and benefits:

Features: _____

Benefits: _____

*The power of accurate observation is
frequently called cynicism by those who don't have it.*

*—George Bernard Shaw (1856-1950)*

# Chapter 3

# Recruit and develop your expatriates

## Executive Summary

- *With an 8-step framework, we help you identify* **2 key selection criteria for
  recruiting expatriates:**
  - *They need to be culturally sensitive, and*
  - *They must be strong coaches.*
- *As you* **share your market research information** *internally, you build strong
  employee communities interested in overseas businesses.*
- *Beware this management issue: Your overseas assignments may not be "success
  tracks" to progressively successful careers–which critically impacts the value of
  your US$30-50 billion annual investment. Solution: Upgrade your handling
  of "expats"—ensure you successfully repatriate them since they are your "first
  team offense" for managing a diverse and inclusive workforce.*

---

*Great things are done by a series of small things brought together.*

—*Vincent van Gogh*

# CHAPTER 3
# WORKSHEET

1. My assessment of the eight-step framework in my company for motivating expats:

|  | Poor | Average | Excellent |
|---|---|---|---|
| • Perform Market Research | _____ | _____ | _____ |
| • Allocate Team Resources | _____ | _____ | _____ |
| • Establish Market Expectations | _____ | _____ | _____ |
| • Select Employees | _____ | _____ | _____ |
| • Customize individual expectations | _____ | _____ | _____ |
| • Sustain home office support | _____ | _____ | _____ |
| • Establish succession plan | _____ | _____ | _____ |
| • Implement successful repatriation | _____ | _____ | _____ |

2. Which Selection Criterion is more important to me:

   a. Technical experts interested in China business and culture _____

   b. Strong coaches interested in developing local talent _____

3. I identify the pool of candidates for overseas assignments by:

   a. Relying on Human Resources _____

   b. Working with an interested employee community _____

   c. Empowering functional supervisors to seek strong candidates _____

   d. Others (specify) _____

4. My biggest headache in identifying well-qualified candidates for expatriate assignment is:

   a. Cost and related benefits _____

   b. Communicating the importance of overseas assignments _____

   c. Others (specify) _____

5. My biggest headache retaining well-qualified expatriates after their assignment is:

   a. Where to put them in the organization _____

   b. Having HR find appropriate assignment for them _____

   c. Others (specify) _____

Key issues I see in recruiting and developing your expatriates:

_____

_____

*It is one of the most beautiful compensations of this life that
no man can sincerely try to help another without helping himself.*

—Ralph Waldo Emerson

# Chapter 4

# Compensation and incentive plans

## *Executive Summary*

- *Your* **incentive compensation is a smaller part** *of your total compensation plan, so motivating expatriates requires long term commitment strengthened by stock options, plus other factors like support for a suitable lifestyle.*

- *Remember:* **Startups of operations depend less on structure,** *more on scheduling and project management. But structure is vital for the long-haul, including a serious focus on compensation plans.*

- *For optimal results,* **ensure you include non-financial incentives** *that include career planning, alongside your financial incentives.*

152

# CHAPTER 4
# WORKSHEET

1. I spend $ _____/year on ___ (#) of US and ___ (#) of Hong Kong/Taiwan expatriates to manage $_____ in sales in China.

2. The average incentive component of the compensation package is ___% of the base pay, or ___% of the total compensation package.

3. My incentive compensation plan includes the following elements:

    a. Startup schedule (if applicable)              ___%
    b. Budget sales/cost/profit/cash flow            ___%
    c. Team building resources                       ___%
    d. Business development                          ___%
    e. Processes/training and targets                ___%
    f. Awards/certifications/community services      ___%
    g. Ethical/compliance                            ___%
    h. Transition/succession plan                    ___%

                                        Total    100 %

4. China is ___ layers of reporting from corporate HQ, and reports to:

    a. Greater China (Hong Kong or Taiwan)     ___
    b. North or East Asia                      ___
    c. Asia                                     ___
    d. Europe                                   ___
    e. Home Office (in US/Europe/Australia)     ___

f. Others (specify_____)    ___

5. How do our comp packages compare to my competitors/peers/customers/suppliers?

___ Above Average        ___ About the same        ___ Below Average

Key issues I see in compensation and incentive plans:

_____

_____

_____

*People talk about the middle of the road as though it were unacceptable.*
*Actually, all human problems, excepting morals, come into the gray areas.*
*Things are not all black and white. There have to be compromises.*
*The middle of the road is all of the usable surface.*
*The extremes, right and left, are in the gutters.*

—Dwight D. Eisenhower

## Chapter 5

# Work-life balance in China-clubs, schools and religion

## *Executive Summary*

- **Expatriates and their families have different needs** *which must be addressed to maximize productivity from your key China-based investment—whether it involves $millions or $billions.*

- *To help your expats,* **target 3 areas to unite expatriate families** *on foreign soil: Clubs, schools and religious communities—all vital to establishing the right work-life balance.*

- **Expats in cities like Shanghai, Beijing and Guangzhou** *require special attention—because of the significantly different living conditions outside these population centers.*

---

*To put the world right in order, we must first put the nation in order;*
*to put the nation in order, we must first put the family in order;*
*to put the family in order, we must first cultivate our personal life;*
*we must first set our hearts right.*

—*Confucius*

# CHAPTER 5
# WORKSHEET

1. In cities like Shanghai, Beijing, Guangzhou, I have _____ expatriate spouses and _____ children who in terms of their living environment, most likely say they are-

   ____Happy ____Neutral    ___Unhappy

2. Outside the major Chinese business cities, I have _____ expatriate spouses and _____ children who, in terms of their living environment, will probably say they are-

   ____Happy ____Neutral    ___Unhappy

3. My company's average tenure for expatriates is _____ years. Of these, _____% of the _____ # of expatriates have families living with them overseas.

   These "average tenure" figures are (check one):

   _____ Significantly higher    _____About the same    _____Significantly below…the percentage of my comparably-ranked employees in the home office. This "turnover differential" tells me how my expatriates' population compares to the home office employees.

4. My expatriates are generally in these segments of the Career Life Cycle:

   ___Segment 1         ___Segment 2         ___Segment 3         ___Segment 4

   (0-5 yrs)         (5-20 yrs)         (20-30 yrs)         (30+yrs)

5. On my visits to China, I normally spend the following amounts of time visiting-

_____ % Customers     _____% at the local office/factory

_____ % Employees    _____% at hotels and/or clubs

_____ % Suppliers     _____% at church

_____ % Others (_____)  _____ % at (_____)

100 % Total        100 % Total

The key issues that challenge my company's expatriate "work-life" balance:

_____

_____

*He who walketh with the wise men will be wise.*

*—Proverbs 13:20a*

# Chapter 6

# Healthy culture and character

## *Executive Summary*

- You have **3** types of culture-*home office, expatriate, and local manage-ment—in China with which* to attract customers, partners, suppliers and employees.

- *To sustain profitable growth,* you want to maintain healthy cultures *that attract equally healthy* communities of business counterparts *(customers, partners, suppliers and employees).*

- "**Strong character**" on your team-*meaning staffers who "do the right things (even) when no one is looking"*-strengthens every level of culture *in your China-based operation.*

*The thing always happens that you really believe in;*
*and the belief in a thing makes it happen.*

*—Frank Lloyd Wright (1869-1959)*

# CHAPTER 6
# WORKSHEET

1. I have ___1 ___2 ___3 culture(s) in China. Strongest in influence is-

    ____Home Office    ____Expatriates ____Local Management

2. I ___advocate ___expect ___ am not concerned whether my employees have:

    a. The "character" to do the "right thing when no one is looking"?
        ___Y ___N

    b. Strong focus on profit, and minimizing cost so long as the company complies with the market and country laws and regulations? ___Y ___N

3. Model companies with strong, healthy cultures for me are:

    _____

4. I communicate culture in the form of:

    _____

5. If I ask my "counterpart community" (my customers, partners and suppliers in China) about my culture, they would say the following:

    _____

Key remaining issues in my company culture and in our character-centric processes:

_____

_____

_____

# Chapter 7

# Managing your local Chinese employees

## *Executive Summary*

- **Skill profile for local Chinese employees***: They're well educated and have varying skills in conversational English. Important: They choose a lifestyle when they join your company and are very willing to learn.*

- **Major motivators for local Chinese employees***: They want to contribute to society, prefer social groupings at work, and they focus on people, not companies.*

- **Your role:** *Stay open minded, use continuous improvement in your thinking to deal with local business practices–e.g., their attitude to sharing salary information.*

*I have found the best way to give advice to your children is to find out what they want and then advise them to do it.*

*—Harry S Truman (1884-1972)*

# CHAPTER 7
# WORKSHEET

1. The three most important reasons why local Chinese join my company are:

   a. _____

   b. _____

   c. _____

2. I think my local Chinese employees can conduct business meetings in English-

   _____ Fluently          _____ Adequately          _____ Poorly

   My solution for this is to: _____

3. I have ways to deal with sensitive local business practices by employees:

   **Local Business Practice**          **My Company Policy**

   #1 Sharing of Salary Information          _____

   #2_____          _____

   #3_____          _____

4. I have several effective ways of recruiting/developing local Chinese employees:

   _____

   _____

   _____

5. My local Chinese employees understand my company culture

___ Well    ___Moderately   ___Inadequately

Key issues I see in my local Chinese workforce:

_____

_____

_____

*Don't judge a man by the words of his mother,*
*listen to the comments of his neighbours.*

*—Yiddish Proverb*

## Chapter 8

# Taiwan and Hong Kong roles in Greater China business

### Executive Summary

- **Taiwanese expatriates fit a profile**: *Entrepreneurially-minded operations managers focused strongly on traditional management techniques, less on management processes.*

- **Hong Kong expatriates represent other skill sets**: *They often are strong in architecture, finance and distribution skills.*

- **Culturally-based practices can interfere with each other**: *Monitor the culture being introduced by Taiwanese or Hong Kong expats. Ensure their focus accelerates growth in China-without divergent from your "home office" practices.*

*A faithful friend is a strong defense: and*
*he that hath found such an one hath found a treasure.*

*—Ecclesiasticus, 6:14*

# CHAPTER 8
# WORKSHEET

1.  I have ＿＿ Hong Kong plus ＿＿ Taiwan expats in my China team responsible for…

    _____

    _____

    For them, I spend US$_____ annually on salaries and development.

2.  We discussed their roles in our China-based operation on _____

    Their biggest concern was _____

    I plan to address this by _____

3.  Future plans for them call for _____

    _____

4.  Key feedback on our Hong Kong/Taiwanese expats, from local Chinese employees: _____

    _____

    We plan to respond to this with the following steps:

    _____

5.  We communicate with our Hong Kong and Taiwan expats in these ways:

    a.  Email          ＿＿%

    b.  Meeting        ＿＿%

c. Telephone     ____%

d. Other     ____% (Specify: _____)

Total     100 %

Key issues I see in my Taiwan and Hong Kong expatriate workforce:

_____

_____

*It's the action, not the fruit of the action,*
*that's important. You have to do the right thing.*
*It may not be in your power, may not be in your time,*
*that there'll be any fruit.*
*But that doesn't mean you stop doing the right thing.*
*You may never know what results come from you action.*
*But if you do nothing, there will be no result.*

—*Gandhi*

# Chapter 9

# Summary

## *Executive Summary*

- *While China is a lucrative market,* **your efforts in China are only as strong as the weakest link**–*your ability to marshal the resources your expatriates need to succeed.*

- **Your most important step now is to successfully repatriate** *your expatriates upon completion of their assignments which will attract strong candidates for future overseas assignments.*

- **Put overseas assignments on the critical path to successful careers** *in your company and create a continuous improvement environment for a global healthy culture that is locally managed.*

*How many a man has dated a new era in his life
from the reading of a book.*

*—Henry David Thoreau (1817-1862)*

# CHAPTER 9
# WORKSHEET

1. The 3 biggest problems I face in China are:

   a. _____

   b. _____

   c. _____

2. My "scouting report" and business intelligence suggests these are **my hurdles:**

   Product barriers _____

   Purchasing barriers _____

   Governmental barriers _____

   Competitor barriers _____

3. The most important strategic case studies for my operations in China:

   Case Study #____ Title: _____

   Case Study #____ Title: _____

4. These strategic cases studies suggest these are the keys for companies like mine:

   _____

   _____

5. My key takeaways from this book are_____

   _____

My next steps in China:

_____

_____

*The doer alone learneth.*

*—Friedrich Nietzsche*

## Chapter 10

# Your "30 Minute Workbook" to build your China ventures

Congratulations! You now have a clear picture of your China business written down in your 9 worksheets. Having completed this process, you are ready for the summary worksheet to help you focus on areas with greatest impact for you.

The core of this systematic, step-by-step approach: With this "30 Minute Workbook" to build your China ventures, you learn the process of building a successful culture in China operations, along with tools to identify the weakest point in your operations performance. Every process has weaknesses and strengths. By focusing on your weaker areas, you improve the entire process–until you find "quality hurdles" based on the evolution of your business.

Welcome to the journey of continuous improvement.

*Think Win Win*

*—Motto for David S. Wu*

# CHAPTER 10
# SUMMARY WORKSHEET

1. I see US$_____ sales and US$_____ profit within _____ years in China (*Chapter 1*).

   I am ___ OK ___not OK as I am at phase ___4 ___5 ___ 6 of Business Life Cycle.

2. I am investing US$_____ in equipment and facility with useful life of _____ years (*Chapter 1*) plus US$_____ per year on ___ number of expatriates to help me get there (*Chapter 4*).

3. My biggest gaps are in the following areas (prioritize as appropriate):

   ____ Resources (funding, sites, equipment, home office support, etc.)

   ____ Strategy and execution (identification, information, process, etc.)

   ____ People managers (recruitment, development, training, succession, etc.)

   ____ People local staff (recruitment, development, training, succession, etc.)

   ____ Partner (supplier, distributor, JV partner, government, etc)

4. My areas of strength are _____ (*Chapter 2*), and motivate my expatriates through _____(*Chapter 3*) who are generally ___performing well ___can do better and are ___satisfied ___dissatisfied.

5. I do not know enough about (prioritize as appropriate)

   ____ My culture in China (*Chapter 6*)

   ____ My local employees (*Chapter 7*)

   ____ My Home Office Expatriates (*Chapters 3, 4, 5*)

   ____ My Taiwan/Hong Kong Expatriates (*Chapter 8*)

6. I will focus on (*Chapter 9*)

    \_\_\_ Research more information on _____

    \_\_\_ Review my business assumptions/expectations regarding _____

    \_\_\_ Review my team specifically in _____areas

My action plan:

_____

_____

_____

*Reading, after a certain age, diverts the mind too much from its creative pursuits. Any man who reads too much and uses his own brain too little falls into lazy habits of thinking.*

*—Albert Einstein (1879-1955)*

## Section V

# Case studies with epilogues

In this segment, you will find 5 case studies, with epilogues.

For confidentiality reasons, company and employee names were changed. "Mark Chen," a composite individual–based on many veteran expatriates with Great China experience–becomes prominent throughout these Case Studies. These are based on actual experiences, and are used to illustrate issues with companies interested in growing globally.

In each instance, you will find these in a Case Study:

- An executive summary of the case
- Relevant background information on the company
- An "org" (organizational) chart and list of key personnel
- Snapshot of the major issues

Through the epilogues, we distill for you the probable next steps and targets. Since the situations captured by our cases occurred at different times, we offer no guarantees that the same conditions exist in the companies under discussion. We can underscore that the situations are drawn from life, and their issues needed resolution.

You're strongly encouraged to independently assess the priorities in each case and highlight the issues most relevant to you.

173

**Note**

If you prefer more information, would like a more comprehensive discussion, or want to customize these cases to your situation, please contact your author, David Wu:

dswu@alumni.princeton.edu or
david.wu.wg82@wharton.upenn.edu

胡氏企業

# Case #1

# T Conglomerate Company©

T Conglomerate Company was founded in 1960 and grew to US$36 billion in sales as a publicly traded company in 2002, mostly through acquisitions in the 1990s. Its high-profile former executives delivered tremendous value to shareholders, but were indicted for looting US$600 million from the company. Ted Greene, the new Chairman and CEO, planned to replace all Board members and restructure T. The stock price declined by over 70% in 2002, the former Director of the Governance Committee pleaded guilty to fraud, and employee shareholders were planning class action litigation to compensate for the loss of their substantial savings, especially in the 401(k) plan.

Ted realized his priorities were to create a team to:

- Establish strong integrity in corporate governance. The process was in place and was proceeding on schedule.

- Establish credibility in financial reporting. The CFO was replaced and the process was proceeding on schedule.

- Affirm market leadership and deliver profitable operations across all businesses. Ted had to focus on a process to make this happen.

175

Looking at his portfolio of businesses, his largest group, Fire and Security, at US$11 billion sales, was also the fastest growing segment. Sustained profitable growth in this business unit would greatly enhance the company's reputation in the investment community. Ted looked at the sources of growth and found Asia to be growing fastest within this fast-growing business unit, approaching US$1 billion sales, mostly out of North Asia, outside Greater China, where the largest market potential was yet to be realized. He wanted to find out the market potential for this fast-growing business unit, especially in Greater China, but his Regional Manager had resigned and left the company.

Ted had to prove his integrity through his new team in order to gain the confidence of investors and employees. He did not have much time, and decided to examine the culture of Greater China for his Fire and Security business while his other priorities proceeded on schedule.

### *T Conglomerate Businesses and Incentive Compensation*

There were five business units until the middle of 2002, when the financing unit TIC was spun off through an IPO. Of the four remaining businesses, Electronics acquired Chemray and PMA to become a global leader in providing connectors and specialty materials. Plastics was for sale but not sold due to weak pricing. Medical was a stable and solid business with leading market positions in disposable medical equipment in the hospital operating room. Finally, Fire and Security was a global leader in both fire and security systems.

As in most large conglomerates, names of the business units can be deceiving. Some products did not naturally fit into these business units. For example, T was the world's largest producer of coat hangers, and a regional leader in car traffic control systems in Hong Kong. These profitable businesses were not visible because they did not have a material impact on the performance of the entire company.

T Conglomerate was not known for astute investments in research and development (R&D). Very few new products were organically developed within the company. Almost all new products were acquired through new businesses. This was largely a reflection of the company culture that rewarded short-term earnings and cash flow. Since it took time to realize the fruits of R&D, which reduced earnings and therefore compensation in the short term, it was far easier for managers to seek acquisitions to achieve immediate higher compensation.

Due to the vertical nature of the business units and the corresponding incentive compensation for managers, synergies across geographic regions were largely ignored. For example, there were 13,000 employees in Greater China across all business units, but each business unit was left to compete amongst themselves. There was very little interaction between the 100 employees of the Fire and Security Business Unit in China and the 12,000 Electronics employees there. The range of joint ventures and acquired businesses was quite diverse, with customers in many industries (e.g., broadband telecommunications infrastructure, semiconductors, pharmaceuticals, cell phones, engineering and construction of retail stores and industrial facilities). Often, different business units bid on the same project and confused the customers, and this was further complicated by acquisitions that were not well communicated within the company.

There were two types of acquisitions:

- Global acquisitions where the acquired company has operations in Greater China.
- Greater China acquisitions with limited scope outside Greater China.

Integration after acquisition was difficult with the volume of acquisitions made, and delivering synergies that required lengthy coordination efforts was not rewarded. Even within the same business unit, it was difficult to deliver synergies due to internal competition for performance. Superior managers focused on customers were not rewarded. Rewards were given to managers who focused on internal politics.

The subjective nature of cost allocations which ultimately delivered the earnings and cash flow associated with individual manager performance was often opaque to the managers themselves. The resulting culture centered on the ability of politician-employees to enhance revenue and divert expenses away from their performance targets.

### Fire and Security Business Unit

A basic contractor support business on a global basis, this US$11 billion operation consisted of 60% services-oriented businesses such as security monitoring services and anti-theft systems, and 40% installation/product sales, where the fire or security system must be put in place especially for new or refurbished buildings. The span of products was even broader in Asia due to acquisitions of labor-intensive guard-force business to support cash-in-transit banking operations, plus traffic control businesses that were acquired to enhanced growth and earnings. Asian acquisitions were generally submitted to the US for approval only, and most of the due diligence activities were performed within Asia.

### ADZ Security Business

ADZ was the world's largest security system provider in a highly fragmented market with over 1 million accounts. Most of the accounts were residential accounts in the US, but there were also governmental and commercial security system customers. In general, this system consisted of sensors at the customer site that communicated via secure connections to a central monitoring station (CMS) staffed 24 hours a day and 7 days a week. At the retail or residential level, the CMS worked with law enforcement agencies such as the police to respond to any break-ins, sometimes after confirmation with the customer. At the commercial level, closed-circuit TVs were installed at strategic locations to monitor activities in any commercial premises, or group of premises, and either local security staff or public law enforcement would respond to any intrusions.

Acquired in 1997, ADZ's growth outside Greater China has been spectacular, but was a non-starter in Greater China. The nature of ADZ was such that a substantial amount of the financial benefits to the company accrue in the first 12 to 24 months of obtaining the account. The basis (presented in Asia): Installation experience established about 100 years ago and accounting procedures recognized as Generally Accepted

Accounting Principles. Initial cash outflow was amortized to deliver higher income through installation fees which were rewarded in the incentive plan. In order for an account to actually generate profit, it must remain active beyond the cancellation period, or three years. In other words, once the decision is made to proceed with CMS operations to support customer accounts, the rate of growth of the customer base must increase. Any time the customer base declines, there would be a much more dramatic impact on ADZ's profitability.

The success of ADZ relied on a combination of direct selling and distributor selling accounts. In both instances a very aggressive manager coordinated a staff usually with high turnover and very focused on obtaining new accounts. In Greater China, software for managing security operations was sold through an independent contractor to the Chinese security organizations such as police precincts, but ADZ was not allowed to participate in CMS operations without governmental approval. In Hong Kong, ADZ obtained the required licenses and a sales manager was in place to run the operations. In Taiwan, ADZ started to operate in 2002.

Greater China largely relied on experience outside Greater China during startup of ADZ. The risks of customer credit-worthiness were largely ignored based on experience outside Greater China, even though litigation with distributors was looming over non-paying customers. An investigation of the process revealed suspicious accounts, most likely due to the tremendous pressure to continue to grow the accounts. The sales manager had job security only when the new accounts grew.

### *Sesmat Security Business*

Starting with licensed amorphous metal technology from ASH in the 1980s, the acousto-magnetic technology based on hysteresis properties was superior to RF technology for anti-theft applications. Most hypermarkets, such as MartWal, used Sesmat products at all store entrances and exits. The basic system was to adhere a tag to the products in the stores to be protected, before the tag was de-activated at the check-out counter. If not de-activated, the tag actuated detector alarms at the entrances or exits.

The alarms alert the store's security staff to apprehend the suspect on the spot. Components of this system included:

- Tags that went on the products. The nature of the acousto-magnetic technology was a "dumb" technology where information could not be stored on these tags. Therefore the focus was to introduce tags at the product production facility instead of the retail outlet or warehouses in between. Almost all tags were manufactured in Puerto Rico, and some in China. The advantage of the competing technology, RF based, was the ability to store information, at the cost of weaker anti-theft capabilities.

- Sensors that detected the tags at entrances and exits. These stands were visible and acted as deterrents, or they were invisible (in the upscale shops) and strictly used as anti-theft devices. This component included the de-activation device at the check-out counter, and the tag detection stand.

- Signal carrier from the sensor to an enforcement activator. This could be an electronic closed-circuit TV similar to the ADZ system, or a simple sound alert system so the check-out counter employees could also act as enforcement officers.

- Apprehend suspect after intrusion detection. This could be the security staff, police department, or others as directed by the security system owner.

Acquired in 2001, Sesmat was a mature global business in need of continued development or the business would lose to more cost-effective competitors. Product tracking using the Global Positioning System to support supply chain management was very important, as was the need to install more tags at the source (production factory), hopefully with stored information to describe the content inside the transportation containers.

### *Fire Business*

T Conglomerate acquired most of the major fire product brands and was the largest fire system provider in the world. The major product offerings were fire detection, alarm, and suppression. There were smoke or heat detectors that trigger a signal to alert the environment that requires attention (such as an alarm for everyone to hear). Depending on the required action, putting out the fire could be manual (e.g., using fire extinguishers) or automatic (e.g., sprinkler systems). For example, every McDonald's in the world has a fire protection system over the kitchen hood that detects fire and can actuate a fire suppression system to protect the facility.

Fire was a mature business, and competition was fierce for new buildings. China, with its sustained 8% annual economic growth over the last decade, was a major frontier for prospective fire business. Different competitors sought advantages to protect their business, including using local manufacturing to reduce import duties and lower the cost of production to be more competitive. The major advantage was lowering the cost of production, and the greatest difference in labor cost was between Japan at US$40 per hour for production workers (including all benefits) and China, at less than US$1 per hour for production workers (including all benefits).

### Greater China Fire and Security Operations

Greater China consisted of Taiwan, Hong Kong, Macau, and China. There was very little coordination among the operations, which were dominated by Hong Kong. China had reported to Hong Kong, and it was impossible to clearly separate China performance from Hong Kong performance based on the financial reports. Taiwan was a relatively small operation, but was growing in importance with the increasing Taiwanese investment in China. The Macau business was very small. With the acquisition of Sesmat, there were significant opportunities to integrate operations and build self-sustaining operations.

### China Fire and Security Operations

Fire and Security operations in China reported to Hong Kong, and were dominated by import of Fire products from Hong Kong. With mixed inventory, it was not possible to isolate China's performance. Ignatius Ng worked for Nick Lam in Hong Kong before being promoted to China operations, and Hong Kong always delivered superior performance while China's performance was erratic. In order to enhance profitability, the China team was directed to declare pressurized containers such as fire extinguisher cylinders as non-dangerous goods to save transportation expenses, and the value of the imported products was declared at lower value to save customs duties and related taxes. Employee expenses were minimized by a combination of substantially reduced benefits, curtailed bonus payments, and very limited training. The resultant culture had very high turnover, and encouraged employees to increase their compensation by soliciting kickbacks from suppliers and distributors. Due to the high turnover, the Hong Kong expatriates did not share the basic product information with the local employees in China, claiming that the Chinese employees can not be trusted. The only information the local Chinese team was allowed to manage was the package price that can be offered to the customers, as long as it is higher than the minimum price specified by the Hong Kong expatriates. Without the basic information on which products were profitable, it was difficult to attract a top-caliber local Chinese team.

In order for Mark to build China operations, these issues had to be addressed, especially in light of Sesmat and other prospective acquisitions.

### *Hong Kong Fire and Security Operations*

Hong Kong operations before the Sesmat acquisition were dominated by Nick Lam, with over 20 years of contracting experience, and an astute manager who clearly understood the driver for financial reporting of income and cash flow. By building a small but very loyal team, the growth through acquisitions was completely eliminated in order to maintain status quo, and he protected the core Hong Kong team. When questions related to inventory valuations arose, there were suspicious activities such as a fire at the warehouse one day before the warehouse was scheduled for a physical inventory count. The small but very loyal team also could not maintain internal control when a group of thieves was able to steal US$300,000 of inventory from the warehouse by forging documentation. At least one employee was arrested for participating in the forged documents, and this was not known to the company until Mark Chen read the Chinese newspapers that reported the incident.

With the Sesmat acquisition, the issues in Hong Kong were:

- People management
- Compensation (including incentive compensation)
- Integrating inherently different Fire and Security operations

### Taiwan Fire and Security Operations

Taiwan operations before the Sesmat acquisition were inflated by acquisition accounting when a previous acquisition price was reduced to allow a higher-than-normal profit margin for contracted businesses post-acquisition. When the contracted businesses were completed, it was not possible to sustain the abnormally high profit, so Fire operations could not sustain its profit growth without additional acquisition accounting.

With Mark Chen managing the integration of the Sesmat acquisition, and a more difficult regulatory environment in the US to drive aggressive acquisition accounting, no anomalies were allowed in acquisition accounting, and the ADZ operations started up in Taiwan at a loss to deliver organic growth.

### Tenure of Mark Chen

Mark was recruited by Hussain Yassaf, who was a very successful Iranian American, and he delivered the highest growth segment for the Fire and Security business unit worldwide. The interview process was limited to the short time for interviews, and driven by Gloria Jason, the Asian Human Resource Director. Mark was not given a chance to meet with his staff prior to his assignment, and relied on Hussain to understand the operations. With the impressive history of acquisitions, Hussain and Mark believed Greater China would grow rapidly. The existing organization was projected to turn into a much smaller part of Greater China, and therefore it was irrelevant who was responsible for the existing organization. As demonstration of good faith, Mark left his family in the US and was stationed in China by himself to accelerate the growth process. It was anticipated that the family would be reunited following a brief transition period after the completion of new acquisitions.

<u>Note</u>

Motivated by the delivery of results to accelerate a reunion with his family, Mark drove the reorganization largely under the leadership and sponsorship of Hussain. The completion of the Sesmat acquisition was completed during Mark's tenure, and additional Letters of Intent were prepared and executed for several acquisitions within 90 days. The acquisition prospect list increased to several hundred quickly, and Mark worked with the Asian acquisition team closely to drive more acquisitions. However, issues at the T Conglomerate US home office began to surface, and the acquisition process was halted before additional acquisitions were completed, leaving the integration of previous acquisitions as the highest priority. Hussain was promoted as part of a re-organization in 2002 to be responsible for Australia, New Zealand, and Europe. Greater China became less of a focus to Hussain, who elected to promote English Hundlum and Michael Straw to be responsible for Asia, supervising Mark Chen.

Without additional acquisitions, Mark focused on delivering growth through synergies and built an effective team. He focused on transparent financial reporting, conducted training for his top managers in Greater China, and provided opportunities for the top managers to interact and get to know all their capabilities. Profitable growth continued, but the rate of growth was limited without additional acquisitions. Seeing lower growth prospects and delayed reunion with his family, Mark contributed to the company's higher growth by resigning and returned to his family.

*Organization*

Exhibit C1-1 is the organization chart of T Conglomerate at the time Ted Greene joined the company. It had vertical organizations on a global basis and geographic organizations in each vertical group. Synergies across businesses were not realized, as compensation packages were driven by specific short term performance.

Ted Greene, the Chairman and CEO, was a Caucasian from outside the company.

## Exhibit C1-1
## T Conglomerate Company Organization Chart

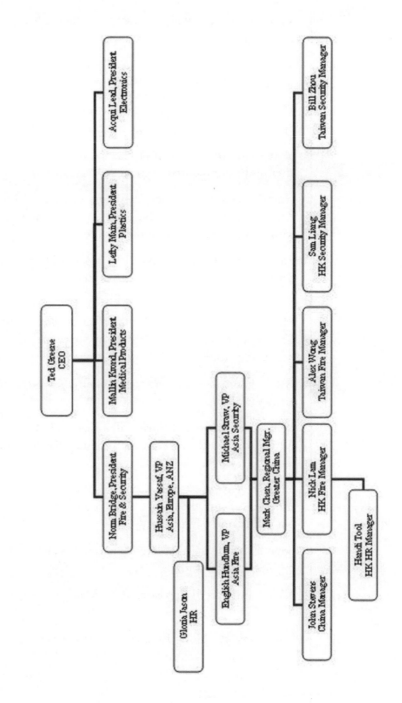

Norm Bridge, the President of Fire & Security, was a Mormon and a star performer.

Acqui Lead, the President of Electronics, was a Caucasian acquired by T Conglomerate in 2000.

Mallin Krond, the President of Medical Products, was acquired by T Conglomerate in a niche market largely left alone.

Lefty Main, the President of Plastics, remained in the company after his business did not attract strategic investors.

Hussain Yassaf, the Vice President of Asia, Australia, New Zealand, and Europe for Fire and Security, was a Suni Muslim with a contracting background for fire systems.

English Hundlum, the Asia VP responsible for Fire, was a British divorcee who expressed his desire to stay in Singapore with his girlfriend and young child.

Michael Straw, the Asia VP responsible for Security, was a Caucasian American just arrived in Singapore with his family and young children.

Gloria Jason, the Asia Human Resource Director, was a local Singaporean.

Mark Chen was the Greater China Regional Manager, an Asian American recruited by Hussain to build Greater China business in 2001.

John Stevens, the China Country Manager, was a Caucasian American divorcee who married a local Chinese and was without children in China.

Ignatius Ng, the China Fire Manager, was an engineer with no business background.

Nick Lam, the Hong Kong Fire Manager, was a local with decades of experience.

Sam Liang, the Hong Kong Security Manager, was a local with decades of retail security experience.

Alex Wong, the Taiwan Fire Manager, was a local Taiwanese with decades of contracting experience.

Bill Zhou, the Taiwan Security Manager, was an entrepreneur who transformed from a US$1 million distributor operation to a US$36 billion company employee within 60 days.

## *The Challenge*

To demonstrate that T Conglomerate could sustain a high-growth business in Asia, Ted wanted to build a successful global culture.

- He had to concentrate on an appropriate compensation plan to motivate his workforce. Heavy emphasis on profit and cash flow had to be balanced by high ethics and integrity. Without checks and balances, he no longer believed high integrity could be expected from the operations with supervision.

- The historical culture of acquisitions had to be transitioned to focus on operational management. While acquisitions could return after restoring shareholder confidence, the acquisitions culture to drive growth in income and cash flow was no longer possible in the immediate future.

- It was a complex challenge to attack all the issues in Greater China simultaneously. Growing the three components of Greater China separately, especially in the absence of acquisitions, made operational sense.

Ted knew that successful execution of this strategy would stabilize investor confidence and add tremendous shareholder value. He was confident that the corporate governance and financial reporting challenges would be accomplished within the next 90 days. If he could concurrently prioritize the issues in delivering sustained high-profit growth, he could accelerate his goal to regain investor confidence.

*A hundred years from now*
*it will not matter what my bank account was,*
*the sort of house I lived in, or the kind of car I drive...*
*but I can rest in peace because I did the right things.*

## Case #1 Epilogue

# T Conglomerate Company©

<u>Note</u>

The company was very successful and grew substantially through the early 21st century, before the US headquarters faced regulatory scrutiny from the government. Acquisitions delivered strong growth in profit and cash flow, but the incentive plan stimulated very aggressive accounting methods, and strongly encouraged short-term behavior. Without a source of funding to sustain acquisition-oriented growth in Asia, many issues related to acquisition accounting, ethics, and integrity surfaced. A complete overhaul of the operating process was required, especially transparent financial accountability.

Acquisition growth focused on higher profit and cash flow on a quarterly basis, forcing the team to sacrifice any actions that took longer than 12 months to materialize. With mature products in its portfolio, sustaining organic growth without synergies was very difficult, and without top managers to advocate and sponsor strong integrity, it would take time for T Conglomerate to re-affirm its market-leading position.

Asia must change its culture to focus more on delivering sustainable profitable growth. The incentive plan must be changed to recognize and reward high integrity behavior and/or longer term investments such as employee training. Without a committed team from the top, it would be very difficult to change the culture.

In one defining moment during Mark's tenure, English Hundlum told him, "We don't want to do things illegally, why do you want to do things right?"

Under these circumstances, Ted decided to replace most of the Fire and Security senior management team in March 2003. This move reinforced his commitment to build the right culture while maintaining his strong market positions. He continues to focus on integrity in corporate governance and credibility in financial reporting.

胡氏企業

# Case #2

# D Conglomerate Company©

Note

D Conglomerate Company was a NYSE-listed company that started from a spin-off of real estate investments circa 1980 with hand tools and instrumentation products. The original owners were astute investors who recruited one of the most respected managers, Tim George, from a tools manufacturer. With strategic acquisitions coupled with a continuous-improvement culture and people development, Tim built one of the strongest growth records on Wall Street with a young team of managers. Benchmarking and improving upon the Japanese management methods, the company customized a Policy Deployment decision-making process for continuous improvement. This process leveraged a set of tools used for training and continuous development. Started from zero, profitable growth of the company approached US$4 billion sales and ~US$500 million cash flow 20 years later, and Tim retired in late 2000. The first employee he hired and continuously developed since the 1980s became the new CEO. As one of the younger CEOs, Larry Young continued to drive and expand upon a young executive management team.

In the early 1990s, Tim drove D Conglomerate into China with a strategic hand tools acquisition and looked for platforms to expand the Instrument and Control businesses. Policy Deployment dictated resources to prioritize opportunities in

Asia. The acquisition of a global instrumentation company, Luke, with a good presence in China, became the platform for entering the 21st century.

Well known for a very small corporate management team, Larry did not have a specific team focused on China acquisitions, and he knew more could be done. As he continued to focus on global strategic acquisitions, China continued to surface in the Policy Deployment decision-making matrix as he contemplated putting more resources to focus on growth there.

### D Conglomerate Businesses

While there were many different strategic acquisitions, the businesses have been grouped as Tools and Non-Tools. The initial core business was supplying Craftsman brand hand tools to Sears; that provided the foundation for creating a continuous-improvement culture and premium market valuation to finance additional strategic acquisitions.

Reflective of Tim's experience, focused tools acquisitions drove globalization while non-tools were more opportunistic acquisitions driving continuous improvement in a broader instrumentation market. A mature mechanical counter business for gasoline stations was a platform for demonstrating profitable growth in a mature industry using Policy Deployment, while other small niche players were amalgamated into the Instrument and Control (IC) Group. With more experience and cash accumulated over time, the company built momentum and became a global leader in the niche market of power tools, and they expanded strategic acquisitions globally beginning in the 1990s.

### Policy Deployment

Exhibit C2-1 was obtained from an investment analyst report showing a sample Policy Deployment Matrix. Policy Deployment was a resource allocation decision-making tool that prioritized opportunities by targets, with resources to support meeting the targets. While there were annual reviews, the process was continuous and flexible to reflect the latest information. The actual implementation of Policy Deployment in a team environment was successful under Tim's leadership in the

## Exhibit C2-1
## Sample Policy Deployment Matrix

| Improve RONA to X% and EBIT to X% | Achieve CAGR of X% | Achieve & Sustain Customer Service Excellence | Achieve & Sustain World Class Product Quality | Improvement Priorities / 3-5 Year Objective / Target To Improve / Benefit | 50% Assembly & Packline Error & Customer Rejection Reduction | 50% Reduction in scrap & rework as a % of transportation cost | Agree on product specs. w/customer 12/92 implement sys to complt at all plants 12/93 | System Approval 4th Quarter 1993 | 95% on time by channel & 100% in 14 days by 7/1/93 | System Approval 4th Quarter 1993 | $XXXX Total Sales in Hardware & Industrial | Monthy plan savings as $ of COGS | Achieve GM as % sales through Price/Mix/Cost reduction | 100% of training plan implemented on schedule | Operations (RESOURCES) | Business Groups (RESOURCES) | EVP (RESOURCES) | Finance (RESOURCES) | Human Resources/DBS (RESOURCES) | MIS (RESOURCES) | Research & Development (RESOURCES) | International (RESOURCES) | Group Executive (RESOURCES) |
|---|---|---|---|---|---|---|---|---|---|---|---|---|---|---|---|---|---|---|---|---|---|---|---|
| O | O | O | O | Define & Implement Formal Training Program | | | | | | | | | | O | O | O | O | O | ● | O | O | O | |
| O | | | | Meet 93 Product Cost Reduction Targets & Gross Margin Targets | | | | | | | | O | O | | ● | ● | O | | | | O | | |
| | O | | | Achieve 1993 Allen Challenge | | | | | | | O | | | | O | ● | O | | | | O | | O |
| | | O | | Define & Develop World Class Customer Service System | | | | | | O | | | | | O | ● | O | | | O | | | O |
| | | O | | Consistently meet on time delivery expectations | | | | | O | | | | | | ● | O | O | | | O | | | |
| | | | O | Define and Develop World Class Quality System | | | O | O | | | | | | | O | O | ● | | | | O | | O |
| | | | O | Improve Product and Packing Quality | O | O | O | | | | | | | | ● | O | O | | | | O | | |

US. The culture that delivered high growth and profits commanded higher valuation premiums from Wall Street analysts. The key challenge was to be included in this team that influenced resource allocation. A sponsor was still required to successfully grow and develop businesses in this environment.

### *D Conglomerate in China*

Following their customers, power tools was the first major strategic investment in China when a Suzhou chuck facility started up circa 1996. Following the new facility investment decision, another strategic acquisition of an Asian hand tools operation headquartered in Taiwan with manufacturing in China for the export market strengthened the Tools business position in China. With the established manufacturing base, the focus in Tools was to explore selling into China in addition to exporting out of China.

IC businesses did not pursue the China market, but sold into China by exporting out of the US or Europe. This started to change when a strategic German acquisition came with a Chinese JV in counters production at Qingdao, and the China market became more attractive with sustained economic growth and WTO entry in 2001.

Policy Deployment, which drove resource allocation, dictated more resources to pursue this attractive market. Since the smaller niche IC businesses did not have the knowledge or resources to pursue this market, a successful Asian American who was already based in Shanghai, Mark Chen, was recruited to drive IC growth in Asia, especially China.

### *China Tools Operation*

The original power tools acquisition was made to support the globalization efforts of D's customers into China. The facility was almost within walking distance of several key customers, and another Asian American was recruited to manage that operation. With global customers already in hand, confidence was high to build and sustain profitable growth in power tools.

The hand tools acquisition in Asia was one of the most strategic acquisitions with extensive negotiations. Atas, a Taiwanese family-owned company with manufacturing operations in China, produced hand tools sometimes under private label to other companies. Tim George negotiated with the Taiwanese owners, convincing the family that the future with global expansion possibilities would be far brighter than continuation as an Asian producer. D Conglomerate absorbed the Atas management completely, and delivered on the commitment to grow competitively in both the Chinese and US markets. The result was a loyal and motivated Asian workforce with a continuous-improvement culture. By acquiring the Taiwanese ownership, D Conglomerate automatically became a strong manufacturer in Chinese production. It was a win-win solution for all parties.

### *The IC Group in China*

Exhibit C2-2 is the organization chart of D Conglomerate at the time Mark arrived. Mark started by establishing a tax-exempt Representative Office in Shanghai to perform market research and perform customer services. After an orientation on Policy Deployment, Mark pursued an operating entity in order to deliver value over time. The first prospective operating entity was the acquisition of the Qingdao JV operation on behalf of the German subsidiary.

Converting the Qingdao JV to a subsidiary would immediately launch D Conglomerate into a leading position in the counter market in China. The counter market includes applications such as counting the number of pages photocopied on a photocopying machine, the number of units of production in a manufacturing facility, etc. Being a leader in this mature business was not very attractive per se, as competition was fierce. Mark coordinated with other IC business unit operating executives to research and prioritize the China market. The developing Chinese economy drove strong demand for infrastructure-related products and services such as power quality and reliability, where the IC Group may have sustainable competitive advantages. Seminars were organized to attract prospective customers and to refine the implementation strategy. Profitable export sales from the US and Europe increased significantly, and

# Exhibit C2-2
## D Conglomerate Company Organization Chart

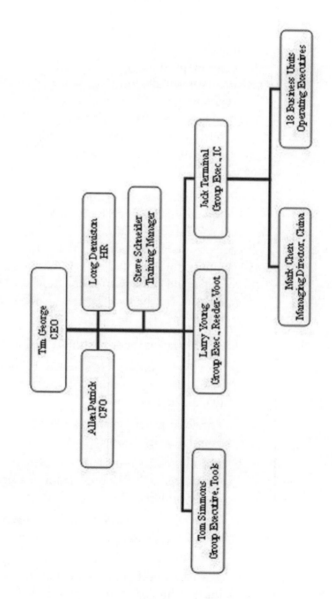

Tim George
CEO

Allen Patrick
CFO

Long Denniston
HR

Steve Schneider
Training Manager

Tom Simmons
Group Executive, Took

Larry Young
Group Exec., Reeder-Voot

Jack Terminal
Group Exec., IC

Mark Chen
Managing Director, China

18 Business Units
Operating Executives

many prospective customers expressed interest in buying the products if there was a local operating entity.

### *Qingdao Due Diligence*

The US$3 million sales Qingdao JV was over-staffed with 200 people, and actually had 250 additional employees on the pension payroll (which included retirees plus other non-working personnel). To reduce the pension payments, the employees on the pension payroll engaged in different revenue-generating activities that actually lost more money than the revenue generated, worsening the financial picture. A typical activity engaged in by the employees on the pension payroll was a chicken farm operation, which had nothing to do with instrumentation products other than perhaps counting the chickens and the eggs on the farm.

Beyond people issues, the mature products did not have sustainable competitive advantage, especially if there was no additional technology and capital infusion. The local general manager was also a major shareholder of the JV, and he financed a large part of his equity through the Chinese government's privatization efforts. Since the Chinese government focused on employment, it was difficult for the local general manager to trim the workforce effectively.

To successfully acquire and grow this Qingdao business, therefore:

- The total equity, assets, selected liabilities, management, financial, and human resources control must turn over to D Conglomerate.
- The local general manager must be replaced by a team from D Conglomerate.
- The new entity must have complete freedom to select its workforce, and this translated into a significantly downsized workforce.
- None of the people and activities engaged by the employees on the pension payroll was to be transferred to the new entity.
- The new workforce must be trained, probably along with more technology and capital infusion.

Jack Terminal visited the Qingdao JV to confirm the agreement on these basic principles. As he returned to the airport after the visit, the airport security guard verbally and physically abused the JV employee who insisted on carrying Jack's luggage to the check-in counter, much to the embarrassment of Jack, Mark, and the Chinese team.

### Benchmark Reeder-Voot Instrument experience in the US

The Qingdao JV produced almost exclusively mature products such as counters for factory machinery and office equipment (e.g., counting the number of pages photocopied in a photo-copying machine). Mark sought to learn more about Policy Deployment in the mature mechanical counter production business in the US under different brand names. He learned that in addition to driving improvements in cost structure to remain competitive, some brands such as Reeder-Voot expanded to provide more systems capabilities to backward integrate to the supply chain management of gasoline to gas stations. This integrated approach used digital technology, and replaced the mechanical counters when the customers changed to digital counters. The business continued to grow, and actually increased customer loyalty as the business grew with the customers.

### Policy Deployment decision on Qingdao acquisition

Tim George, Allen Patrick, Jack Terminal, and Mark Chen met to discuss whether to proceed with the Qingdao JV acquisition. The general consensus was:

- Entering the China market as the leading counter manu-facturer, a mature market, competing on price may not be the best entry strategy.

- There were likely more attractive acquisition candidates available.

The meeting ended with a negative decision on the Qingdao acquisition, and Mark was charged to seek more acquisition candidates, working with business unit operating executives and the Corporate Development group.

**Note**

### *Luke and Other Acquisition Candidates*

Mark continued to identify, prioritize, and perform due diligence on several attractive acquisition candidates with infrastructure-related products. However, it was becoming more difficult to organize the business units to drive the acquisition process. Jack Terminal never returned to China after his visit to Qingdao. Without Jack's sponsorship, the support for China further dwindled.

Meanwhile, D Conglomerate continued to make strategic acquisitions worldwide. One of the acquisitions, Luke, had a strong presence in China. After supporting the completion of the Luke acquisition, Mark met with Jack and the Luke executives. It was determined that IC Group was not ready to dedicate more resources to grow. Mark left the company soon afterwards.

### *Organization*

Exhibit C2-2 is the organization chart of D Conglomerate at the time Mark Chen joined the company. It had a vertical organization on a global basis, and Mark was the first manager to focus on growing the businesses geographically.

Tim George, the CEO, was a Caucasian male from the tools industry.

Allen Patrick, the CFO, was a Caucasian male from Arthur Anderson.

Long Denniston, the HR Director, was a Caucasian male based in Connecticut.

Steve Schneider, the Policy Deployment Training Manager, was a Caucasian male based in Connecticut.

Tom Simmons, Group Executive of Tools, was a Caucasian male based in Connecticut.

Larry Young, Group Executive of Reeder Voot, was a Caucasian male and a Harvard MBA graduate based in Connecticut.

Jack Terminal, Group Executive of Instrument and Control Group, was a Caucasian male based in Connecticut.

Mark Chen, Managing Director of China, was an Asian American based in Shanghai.

The 18 business units were scattered through the US and Europe, each with an operating executive reporting to Jack Terminal. The businesses were related to power quality and reliability, motion controls, temperature/pressure and related process control instrumentation, and aerospace fire suppression systems, among others. The businesses ranged from US$1 million sales to US$100 million sales each.

## *The Issue*

Should Larry Young focus more resources on China growth?

# Case #2 Epilogue

# D Conglomerate Company©

Note

D Conglomerate has a very successful culture of continuous improvement in the US. Its growth continued from the previous strategic acquisitions in China. It focused on global acquisitions with Chinese operations instead of looking at China as a strategic market. Without a leader to drive the Policy Deployment culture in a different language and environment, growth in China remained opportunistic rather than strategic. If the glass were half empty, the depressed economy in 2002-3 was not the right time to focus on strategic growth in China. If the glass were half full, it was the perfect opportunity. The driver could come from Wall Street's lower stock valuation premium. Already, the stock price has become more volatile, although the poor US economy was undoubtedly partially responsible for the volatility.

Policy Deployment drove performance objectively, but it missed profitable opportunities because the decision-makers were a homogeneous group of executives. Larry Young was strongly committed to young Caucasian males in his team because that was his background. He lacked diversity in top management to capture strategic opportunities and sustain profitable growth.

Mark Chen was given the responsibility of Asia/China at a great distance away from the home office. Jack Terminal gave a low priority to pursuing this market. After Mark's departure, it was revealed that Jack had cancer, and he passed away soon afterwards. Without sponsorship from the home office team, it was not possible for Mark to succeed. Unfortunately, Jack's last images of China were very negative, and he never returned to China after his visit to Qingdao.

D Conglomerate continued to succeed with Policy Deployment. The elite Caucasian culture became a bigger barrier for others, and began to miss strategic acquisition opportunities. Larry Young has been seeking to create a win-win solution by adding and developing a more diverse team to deliver growth in Asia, mindful that he himself had been developed by Tim George for over a decade.

胡氏企業

# Case #3

# ASH Conglomerate Company©

Note

ASH Conglomerate Company was one of the Dow components, after growing from a US$1 billion sales chemical company in 1980 to a US$25 billion conglomerate by 2001. The company grew mostly through acquisitions, reaching US$12 billion sales by 1991 when the Vice Chairman of another conglomerate, Larry Bea, was recruited to deliver shareholder value. The stock soared through the 1990s before he created ASH and transitioned his responsibilities to David See.

It seemed ASH was always restructuring. US$900 million was written off for restructuring in 1991. More write-offs followed in subsequent years. Even though restructuring, mergers and acquisitions made it difficult to compare operating performance; it was not important since shareholders' perception of value remained strong and earnings continued to grow.

As David See prepared for another round of layoffs, he was looking at the prospects of sustaining earnings growth while maintaining a strong and dedicated workforce. He had to balance several key global trends:

- Military sales–attractive as President Bush prepared for war with Iraq. However, who can openly support warfare?
- China market potential–the most populous nation entered the WTO in 2001, and presented many profitable business

opportunities. ASH has been in China for two decades. This was an opportunity to illustrate superior management, but ASH had to have the processes in place to deliver.

- Integration–with the convergence of telecommunications equipment, basic product manufacturing faced fierce competition. A market differentiator might be advancing systems integration, where few players compete. However, the business environment was depressed and the market reception to a push for system integration was probably negative.

David See decided to examine his processes to identify key attributes he had to reinforce to ensure success with a stronger global presence.

### *Financial Performance Measurement*

With the guiding principle of creating clear, understandable metrics that can be tied to compensation, David See started by looking at the ASH experience in this area. He found that when Larry Bea was the Chairman in 1991, he started a process to review the entire business portfolio. He carried with him specific financial performance measures in order to compare completely different businesses and to prioritize opportunities. The following productivity concept was very simple and easy to understand:

For any business or business segment, calculate the following quotient using this year's financial information and call this "Year 1 Quotient": (Revenue/Cost). Then calculate the same quotient using last year's financial information, adjusted for inflation factors, and call this "Year 0 Quotient." The productivity was the ratio of "Year 1 Quotient" divided by "Year 0 Quotient."

In layman's terms, this calculated the increase in revenue that can be delivered year after year for a given dollar of expense. This productivity measure was first reported in the 1992 annual report. While there were inherent limitations, it was an excellent communication tool that evolved to more advanced systems such as Six Sigma, and formed the foundation for a continuous-improvement culture.

Looking at the financial performance of ASH operations in China, the first profitable investment was reported in 1995, and not many investments were profitable. Therefore, one option was to develop this financial measure for China operations.

### The Only Profitable Investment in China in the 20<sup>th</sup> Century

David See was surprised to see that the first profitable investment was reported only in 1995, and there was only one profitable investment in China between 1995 and 2000. He decided to take a closer look. He found that an employee named Mark Chen, an Asian American from Ivy League schools, was responsible for this profitable investment after joining the ASH Corporate Operations Analysis Department in 1992. It turned out that he drove the implementation of the productivity financial performance measure throughout the company, and pointed out a weak ASH presence in Asia. The company assigned him to develop businesses in Asia, and he successfully identified the partner and negotiated the majority-owned joint venture with a Chinese customer who not only purchased ASH products, but also committed 100% of the aftermarket business to the joint venture. (The joint venture was negotiated before the Chinese government prohibited foreign enterprises from being the majority shareholder in the aerospace industry, and this ownership structure can not be repeated until the relevant provisions in the WTO are implemented, probably after 2005. Mark managed the joint venture until it was fully certified and became profitable, but a scheduled visit by Larry Bea was cancelled, and Mark left the company soon afterwards.

### Internal Study Findings

Mark's JV was the most profitable by far among the 40+ ASH venture investments in China. David See directed a study on the circumstances that led to the success of Mark's investment. A summary of the report follows:

Mark Chen was assigned to the Aerospace Equipment Business Unit as Director of Asian Business Development, responsible for seeking and growing profitable business opportunities. This was a US$2 billion business unit in 1992 with many proprietary products and services. At that time, the business unit had air-craft engine accessories, interior cabinet components, cockpit avionic accessories, and aircraft landing systems, including maintenance, repair, and overhaul (MRO) services. Aircraft landing systems (ALS) was among the most profitable opera-tions of the entire ASH company, and the MRO services were an extension of product manufacturing. There were only three major ALS manufacturers in the world, and some ALS products had to be serviced by the original manufacturers, or the end user could lose the product warranty, which was very valuable. The nature of the ALS business was to give away the products when the end users purchased the aircraft initially, and the entire profit was based on replacement parts and related services such as MRO.

As part of an effort to sell ALS products, Mark joined the Sales team in China. He reported that the customer strongly sup-ported a MRO JV, and could be quite flexible on terms. His supervisor directed Mark to lead the JV discussions as part of the selling effort to the customer. The personnel files showed a fax from the Chinese customer stating that they selected ASH products largely because a Letter of Intent (LOI) to establish a JV was signed, and ASH was sincere in helping this customer reach international flight standards.

Mark was fully responsible for leading a team of negotiators to deliver the JV consistent with ASH terms. Mark negotiated in Chinese, taking eight months to fully negotiate a four-inch-thick contract written in Chinese and English, approved by ASH management, the JV partner, and another four months to obtain the business license from the Chinese government. The JV partner requested that Mark drive the recruitment, training, and certification of the JV. After group interviews to recruit the entirely local workforce, the training was con-ducted in US facilities within four months, and the procure-ment and plant layout were done concurrently, allowing the facility to start up within two months of the completion of training. The JV achieved US and Chinese government certifi-cation approvals, ISO9002, High Technology Enterprise, and other awards during startup, and profit was reported within the first three months of operations.

Mark's speed of accomplishment was a major embarrassment to the other 16 teams negotiating or starting up ventures in China at that time. When Mark visited Larry Bea with the JV partner, Larry indicated he would visit the JV during his next visit. Due to various reasons, Larry's next visit to Asia did not include a visit to Mark's JV. Mark resigned soon afterwards.

The JV partner was upset that ASH allowed Mark to leave, and the relationship was tense for over six months. ASH proposed several candidates that were rejected by the JV partner. Finally, an outsider with 30+years of non-aerospace experience was recruited as a caretaker of the JV.

### *The Organization*

Exhibit C3-1 is the organization chart of ASH at the time the JV was created. It is a matrix organization, with International managing geographically, and line managers managing offerings of products and services. Each Operating Unit was supported by Human Resources staff that provided input to the Management Resource Review up to the Corporate Senior Vice President of Human Resources.

Larry Bea, the Chairman and CEO, was a Caucasian from another conglomerate company.

George Most, the CFO, was a Caucasian responsible for Corporate Development and Operations Analysis, in addition to both Treasury and Controller functions.

Donald Friend, the HR Senior Vice President, was a Caucasian with over 25 years ASH experience, with expertise on union issues.

Schindler Jones, the President of ASH International, was a French citizen born in Vietnam, specializing in government relations.

Ronald Zhang, the VP of Greater China, was an Asian American with expertise in Chinese culture. He was an important member of Mark's negotiations team.

### Exhibit C3-1
### ASH Conglomerate Company Organization Chart

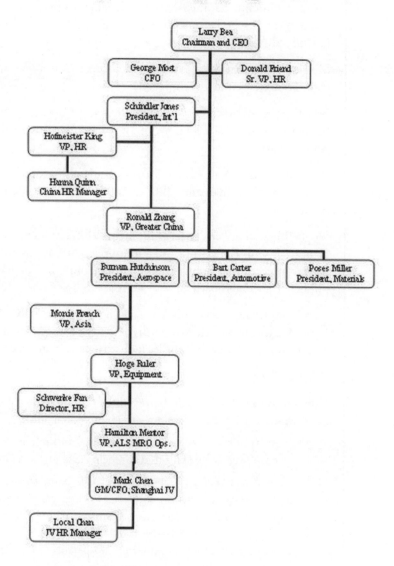

Hofmeister King, the HR VP of International, was a Caucasian more familiar with union issues than different cultures. He inherited from his predecessor the HR Manager of China, Hanna Quinn, a Caucasian female, who left soon after Mark Chen left ASH.

Burnam Hutchinson, the Aerospace President, was a Caucasian star performer who became the Chairman and CEO of another Fortune 500 company.

Monie French, the VP of Asia for Aerospace, was a Caucasian from France based in Tokyo, Japan.

Bart Carter, the Automotive President, was a Caucasian with a financial background, and became an executive in a private equity entity.

Poses Miller, the Materials President, was a Jewish executive who became the Chairman and CEO of another Fortune 500 company.

Hoge Ruler, the Aerospace Equipment Vice President, was a Caucasian who came from the automotive parts industry, and has returned to that industry as Chairman and CEO of a small publicly traded company.

Hamilton Mentor, the Aircraft Landing Systems MRO Vice President, was a Caucasian who worked as a McKinsey consultant, and became the CEO of a smaller industrial parts manufacturer.

### *The Challenge*

Convinced that ASH can do better in the China market, David See devised a structure to build a successful global culture:

- Identify, attract, recruit, train, develop, and retain a team of employees with skills that can help ASH grow in China.

- Find career paths for members of this team so overseas assignments are not impediments to their career growth. In other words, an overseas assignment is not a one-way street. There must also be room for local employees to grow based on their capabilities and performance. Career paths are not limited to US employees.

- Develop culturally sensitive executives to grow in other parts of the world, such as India, Africa, and South America, leveraging the lessons learned in Asia.

He asked his new Senior Vice President of Human Resources to develop metrics not only for financial performance, but also to relate financial performance to the diversity of the management team and the team's interactions. After the initial review within 30 days, David planned to develop and communicate the success attributes, along with a path to succeed.

The target date to begin the execution of this initiative was 60 days, with measurable results for comparable studies beginning as soon as possible.

*If you work hard enough,*
*You can grid steel rods to make needles.*

*—Chinese Proverb*

## Case #3 Epilogue

# ASH Conglomerate Company©

With the right team, success can be achieved in China quickly and profitably. With FAA-approved products, Mark Chen's profitable investment was an opportunity for ASH to launch a successful culture. When Mark left, the ASH image, reputation, and brand value were diminished, which could cost millions of dollars. Local employees focused on delivering results became disillusioned and maintained status quo with the caretaker manager. ASH had to identify and capture the next opportunity to launch a successful culture.

David See decided to focus on building a global diversity effort to retain valued employees, and he made it a global initiative instead of a regional initiative in China. Two dimensions were considered:

- HR had to work with Operations to support core values consistently and deliver continuous improvement. The processes of "Management Resource Review" and "Integrated Performance Management and Development" were revised to have shared ownership between HR and Operations.

- A team of change agents were introduced to continue the re-structuring, since the merger that created ASH significantly increased the revenue base worldwide, including China. This team of continuous-improvement managers also served as ombudsmen for the employees worldwide.

Benchmarking AT&T, ASH also stimulated the development of employee groups to reinforce and support the value of diversity. For all employees interested in an Asian career, Asian managers were invited to speak in the employee gatherings to share "the front-line perspective" on businesses in that region of the world. This became a natural pipeline to develop employees, and was a win-win situation.

Reorganization and restructuring have been a constant in ASH. The next priority for David is the balance between constant change and stability. In this instance, both the International staff and the Operations staff were replaced and the evolution continued.

胡氏企業

# Case #4

# Genteli Telecom Company©

Note

Genteli was one of the fastest rising and fallen stars in the Internet bubble, as company valuations skyrocketed, exploded, and crashed down to earth. From start-up operations in the mid-1990s, it reached a billion-dollar valuation by 2000 and did not accept additional funding offered by both investors and bankers. Genteli's President, the former AT&T President Mandel Alexander, commanded credibility in the new technology and was destined to replace AT&T in the 21st century. Focused on expanding the network instead of obtaining customers, the company was highly leveraged, and ran into cash-flow problems when the stock valuations no longer supported the debt burden.

Aku Dooraty, Vice President of International Development, drove the development of global joint ventures (JV) in Europe, Latin America, and Asia. At various stages of development for his JVs with coverage in Korea, Hong Kong, Argentina, France, Spain, and Germany, he successfully obtained a government license with a Hong Kong partner in 2000. US$6.4 million was deposited as part of the procedures to obtain the Hong Kong license, but the JV did not look like it could meet the milestones specified in the license, and stood to lose US$6.4 million in bond deposit. When his M&A Director introduced Mark Chen to him, Aku actively recruited Mark to join Genteli as Vice

President of Asian Operations and Chief Operating Officer of the Hong Kong JV to grow the business.

Mark Chen was convinced to join Genteli less than six months before Genteli declared bankruptcy. The offices were closed except for a skeletal crew to support the existing customer base in the US.

Successful assignments required commitment from both the employer and the employee. In this instance, the process of obtaining information during interviews was presented for discussions.

## *Telecommunications Industry*

The ability to mass communicate was one of the greatest achievements of mankind in the 20th century. There is no dispute that the amount of time required to communicate with most of the 6 billion people on earth in 2001 was incredibly shorter than in 1901.

In the 21st century, optical technology will likely replace electric copper wiring technology to allow digital video broadband technology into our homes. Wireless technologies, especially satellite based, will create more global coverage with less infrastructure.

In the US, Bluetooth (also known as 802.11(b) technology) already exists, and emerging technologies such as pulse-based digital Ultra Wide Band (UWB, or Wireless Personal Area Network (WPAN) with prospective 802.15.3 specifications and 803.15.3 documentations) received Federal Communications Commission limited license in early 2002. If there was a UWB-based cellular phone network, the network would be naturally encrypted, requiring very little power (and therefore very long battery life in the order of magnitude of several months instead of several hours), and could have instant video and precision location with movement sensors automatically tied to wireless PDA and PC video networks.

In China, almost all cables installed in the last decade have been fiber-optic cables. Telecommunications infrastructure investments have averaged US$20-30 billion per year. The public optical network, mostly controlled by China Telecom, consists of eight horizontal east-to-west trunk lines and eight vertical north-to-south trunk lines. This network covers all 31 provincial capitals (see Exhibit C4-1). According to China's Five-Year Plans, the long-distance transmission network will comprise a fiber-optic trunk cable stretching over 200,000 km, a microwave trunk of 140,000 km, and 40 large-scale satellite earth stations.

There are many components required to support an effective fiber-optic network. A commonly used figure of merit for communications systems is bit-rate-distance (i.e., BL) product (measured in bits/sec-kilometer or bps-km), which measures the speed and distance before additional components such as repeaters have to be added or the signal (i.e., information) would be lost. This distance has increased exponentially, making fiber-optic systems economical, viable, and attractive. The current technology is to use wavelength-division multiplexing (WDM) to increase the bit/sec rate and erbium-doped fiber amplifiers to actively make the signal stronger, and therefore never lose a signal under ideal circumstances. These developments have a dramatic impact on the figure of merit for optical communications systems. By comparison, the BL for telephones was about 1000 bps-km in 1901. The BL for current optical systems with WDM and erbium-doped fiber amplifiers is about 1,000,000,000,000,000 bps-km in 2001, one-trillion times faster and/or longer than in 1901!

Guess what? Some erbium-doped fiber amplifiers are assembled in China today in a joint venture with Corning.

While the most common equipment we use at home today is still the 56k modem, "high speed" is considered very fast at T-1 speed of 1.5 megabyte/sec, or over 20 times the speed of the 56k modem. China has already demonstrated 155.52 megabyte/sec purely optical network communications between Beijing and Shanghai, about 1,000 miles apart (Optical Carrier Level 3 or OC-3 in the Synchronous Optical Network, or Synchronous Transport Mode Level 1 or STM-1 in the Synchronous Digital Hierarchy or SDH). Speeds as high as 10 gigabytes/sec optical transmission technologies have been demonstrated in portions of this network in 2000 (see Kathleen Richards' article in:

**Exhibit C4-1**
**China's Optical Network**

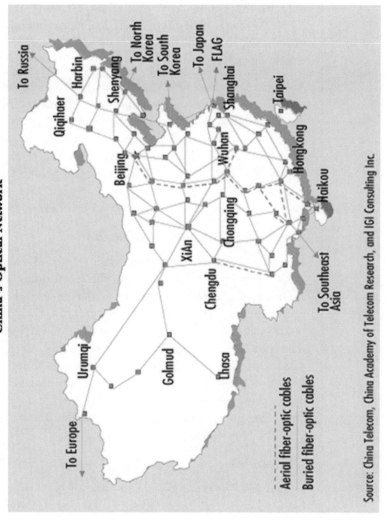

Aerial fiber-optic cables
Buried fiber-optic cables

Source: China Telecom, China Academy of Telecom Research, and IGI Consulting Inc.

Note

http://www.fiber-
exchange.com/archives/coverstory/cstory_1100.htm).

China Telecom, the dominant carrier in China, operates the second-largest SDH network in the world, and China is second
only to the US in its Dense Wave Division Multiplexing
(DWDM) implementation. When satellite communications are
introduced, there will be another major influx of information
technology advancement.

An immediate short-term problem with broadband technology
was how to carry the information from the hub or outlet to the
home. This "last mile" of connection typically required cables to
be installed underground, which was an expensive and time-
consuming process. Instead of cables, there were several wireless
alternatives, one of which was Local Multipoint Distribution
System, or LMDS, which completed the last-mile broadband
access without installing wires among buildings.

### Genteli Telecommunications Technology

Genteli was a wireless voice and data integrated operator that
leased the fiber infrastructure from the major providers such as
WorldCom, adding equipment from companies such as Nortel
and Hughes, with switches from companies like Cisco to create a
LMDS network for customers. At the heart of the network were
transceiver antennae, usually on top of buildings, that communicated with each other. Depending on usage, 4-6 megabytes per
second of information could be telecommunicated within a five-
mile radius, sometimes up to 12 miles when the weather was
clear. The range decreases with poor weather, and therefore the
practical range of antennae was usually shorter.

### Organization

Exhibit C4-2 is the organization chart of Genteli at the time
Mark Chen joined the company. It has a vertical organization
on a global basis, managed by the home office in Vienna,
Virginia.

Mandel Alexander, the CEO, was a Caucasian male and former
President of AT&T.

## Exhibit C4-2
## Genteli Telecom Company Organization Chart

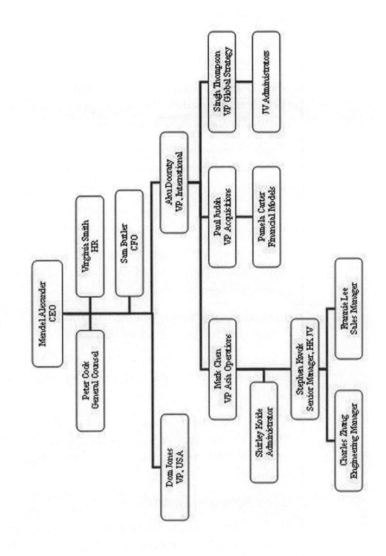

Peter Cook, General Counsel, was a Caucasian male and former MCI General Counsel.

Virginia Smith, the HR Director, was a Caucasian female based in Vienna, Virginia.

Dom Jones, the Domestic Vice President, was a Caucasian male based in Vienna, Virginia.

Aku Dooraty, International Development VP, was an African-British male based in Vienna, Virginia. He was a leading sales person for Cable & Wireless in the US and Europe.

Singh Thompson, VP Global Strategy, was an Indian American male responsible for the financial strategy of the international group.

Paul Judah, VP of Acquisitions, was a Jewish American male responsible for acquisitions negotiations.

Mark Chen, VP of Asia Operations, was an Asian American male responsible for the Hong Kong JV, supported by Shirley Koide, JV Administrator.

Stephen Kwok, Senior Manager of the Hong Kong JV, represented the Hong Kong partner in the JV.

Charles Zhang, Engineering Manager of the Hong Kong JV, was responsible for the technical performance of the Hong Kong network.

Frannie Lee, Sales Manager of the Hong Kong JV, was responsible for the sales performance of the Hong Kong business. She was also the Chairwoman of the Hong Kong online retailers association.

### *Hong Kong Joint Venture*

The Hong Kong government's Office of Telecommunications Authority issued four licenses for the LMDS spectrum in 1999 with great fanfare. 300 MHz bandwidth was awarded to the Genteli-TCC JV and a US$6.4 million performance bond was deposited with the Hong Kong government authorities as a good-faith commitment to deliver the network. With a peak payroll of 54 people, eight buildings were established as a demonstration network, and a network center was being established to coordinate the traffic in 2001. The business was projected to approach a US$200 million operation by the year 2010.

The 2001 goals were ambitious as the Sales Manager Frannie Lee focused on both selling to ISPs (i.e., wholesale), and directly selling to individual customers in a building (i.e., retail). The network had to be very big in order to accommodate both sets of customers. The COO was not able to focus on starting up operations and resigned. The JV was at risk of missing performance bond milestones.

### *Finding/Recruiting Mark Chen*

Mark was a successful Asian American with strong academic credentials who spent four years managing Greater China businesses, including the delivery of yellow-page electronic content to the cellular phones. An introductory meeting with the VP of Acquisitions led to meetings with Aku Dooraty, Peter Cook, and Mendel Alexander, all with tremendous telecommunications credentials fit for a very successful business. A former President of AT&T, coupled with the former General Counsel of MCI, leading a US$200 million start-up operation where a European Sales executive from Cable & Wireless was leading International Business Development. Within the previous 24 months, the company rejected a US$500 million infusion from investors, and had "several hundred millions" of cash to sustain growth, despite the steep drop in market price from US$100 per share to US$6 per share.

Mark talked to the former Manager of the Hong Kong JV negotiations who resigned to join Booz Allen Hamilton. He learned from The Wharton School that the company had recruited successfully there. He also met with the Hong Kong team to obtain a better understanding of the issues, and a prospective wholesale customer/ISP gave encouraging feedback. The general message was the need to focus and deliver results. The business shall be there! Committed to delivering results, Mark joined Genteli in early 2001.

**Note**

### *Reality*

Within one month of joining Genteli, Mark removed the sales and marketing team focused on selling to retail customers, and organized a team focused on wholesale or ISP customers. With the focus on wholesale operations, the network specification was delivered within six weeks, and a meeting with the network equipment vendor accelerated the delivery of the appropriate equipment to meet the next milestone.

Unfortunately, there was no funding to pay the vendor for the network equipment. The Hong Kong partner refused to increase their exposure in this venture, knowing Genteli faced liquidity problems and could face bankruptcy. In fact the Hong Kong partner was quite astute and Genteli was not able to provide more funding for the JV. When the JV received funding through meeting the next milestone, the Hong Kong partner claimed possession of the funds to pay off the inter-company accounts, and the JV had no operating capital to continue operations.

Within six months of Mark's initial contact with Genteli, Genteli declared bankruptcy and was sold. The JV ceased operations due to the lack of funds, and all employees were released.

# Case #4 Epilogue

# Genteli Telecom Company©

<u>Note</u>

The Theory of Efficient Markets applies in this particular case, as Mark ignored the following evidence that this assignment was risky:

- The steep drop in the stock price.

- The resignations of the team members in both Hong Kong and the US.

Instead of being enamored with the industry and technology, the general investing public was wise in anticipating the demise of the company.

After Genteli declared bankruptcy, another telecommunications company acquired Genteli, and is preparing a Business Plan to emerge out of bankruptcy. The LMDS network has been significantly downsized to be commensurate with the customer base, and there is ongoing litigation on the legality of the downsizing taken by the new owners.

胡氏企業

# Case #5

# ABC Printing Company©

Note

ABC Printing Company was one of the largest and oldest printing companies in the world, publicly traded in the NYSE. It prints over 50% of top selling US magazines and ~80% of New York Times best selling novels. It is a global leader in financial printing such as prospecti for Initial Public Offerings and it is the world's largest printer of yellow pages with 20% global market share. About 100 years ago, ABC started as a family business with publishing and printing. A cousin of the family separated the publishing operation ~70 years ago, and it became a pure printer. The last one of the family members retired from the Board of Directors in 2000, even though the family still owned about 15% of the company.

The market share and profitability have been declining over the recent years, mostly because of competition, and new ways to communicate proliferated–Internet, video, cellular telephones, etc. The major European competitors such as Bertelsmann largely dominate Europe. The key market yet to be fully explored was Asia where many fragmented small businesses dominate different niches of the business.

Bill Walter, Chairman and CEO, wanted to transform ABC to a multimedia communications solutions provider based on:

- ABC's ability to grow beyond printing, and
- Capture the Asian market.

However, the progress has been slow. ABC missed the Internet bubble after it sold QuestMap. Although ABC was the first major foreign printer to enter China in the early 1990s with a 90+% ownership of a JV, the JV was never profitable except 1999-2000, and returned to losing money when the decision was made to invest in a new web press and a second JV. The second JV was a high-risk investment for a minority ownership, and Bill was managing through a recession while President Bush prepared for war against Iraq. As Bill traveled to China, his Asia President just left the company, and he was thinking about his growth strategy in Asia.

### *Printing Industry*

Printing was a $200 billion global industry, depending on how the industry was defined. Anyone with a personal computer, word processing software, and a printer can print. With a good photocopying machine and a sorter, the volume can increase to several thousand copies. With digital machines that were still expensive on a per page basis, several hundred thousand copies of customized brochures, books, newsletters or magazines can be printed. Offset printing with a web press was the most popular mode for high volume printing. Gravure printing was common for the best quality and highest volume jobs such as National Geographic magazines. The printing industry is defined by offset printing. Businesses such as Kinko were not considered part of this industry.

There were not many pure printers in this industry, as the growth prospects were perceived to be limited with the advent of the "paperless society." Key players such as Bertelsmann have diversified into e-books, publishing, and Internet commerce. Small niche players dominated this industry, usually not with the fastest or the most advanced web press. With the cost of digital printing rapidly declining, the available market for web printing was also declining. However, there were spots of growth. For example, with the arrival of computer games and new Internet features, the printed books and magazines to support new features and strategies for computer games have increased.

### *Printing Process*

Even though printing was invented by the Chinese several thousand years ago, the technology of printing has evolved in the last 30 years to web printing due to factors related to cost, quality, consistency, and timeliness. Two key steps were required to support web printing:

- To prepare the content on the web press, a process called Pre-Media converted content onto plates that go on the printing web.

- After web printing, a process called binding cut the printed pages, assemble them into a book and glue or stitch the pages together before the cover was inserted to make the final product.

In the US, ABC took mostly electronic content from the publishers, and converted the electronic content onto plates for printing. Protected by copyright and other intellectual property rights, the publishers owned this content. Albeit over one quadrillion (i.e. million billion) bytes of electronic content was managed by ABC, very little of the content was owned by ABC. On any given day, many terabytes (thousands of billions of bytes) of electronic content moved around secured servers in preparation for printing.

Web printing was capital intensive. Each new web press cost about US$3-7 million, and can increase pending on installation, spare parts, and training requirements on the web press in addition to Pre-Media and binding operations. The newer presses have more automation, higher speed, better quality control, etc. However, a well maintained web press could run 40-50 years. With experienced operators, the quality of the printed product was difficult to differentiate from a layman's perspective. Because the web press was so expensive, the business was most profitable when the press was operating 24 hours a day, seven days a week. The profitability of a printing operation normally was highest after the web press has been fully depreciated.

## *The Organization*

Exhibit C5-1 was the organization chart of ABC in the late 1990s. Each Business Unit was supported by Human Resource Specialists who were members of the Human Resource Committee chaired by the Corporate Human Resource Senior Vice President. Each Business Unit has many printing facilities and Human Resource Specialists with dotted line reporting relationship to the Business Unit Human Resource Specialist.

Bill Walter, the Chairman and CEO, was a Caucasian from outside the printing industry.

Francis Kellogg, the CFO, was the highest-ranking female responsible for Corporate Development and Public Relations, in addition to both Treasury and Controller functions.

Dealer Detroit, the HR Senior VP, was an African American who owned several car dealerships before being recruited to ABC.

Ward Hutchinson, the COO, was a Caucasian career printer who was committed to printing. He was a conservative businessman who supported the CEO in the execution of programs. He left ABC to become CEO of another printing company in 2000.

Daly Jones, the Telecommunications President, started as a proofreader and was the highest ranking African American line manager. He has been a star performer, and took the leadership position in both pursuing multimedia opportunities and China operations. He left the company in 2002 to become CEO of a printing equipment company.

Quinn Move, the Telecommunications Senior Vice President, was a Caucasian career printer with over 30 years printing experience, responsible for International Business in Telecommunications. He was stationed in South America as an expatriate in the magazine division before his transfer to this assignment after the South American operation was shut down.

Lawler Smith, the Magazines President, was a Harvard graduate and a lawyer by training. He has taken the leadership of pursuing Pre-Media opportunities for ABC.

## Exhibit C5-1
## ABC Printing Company Organization Chart

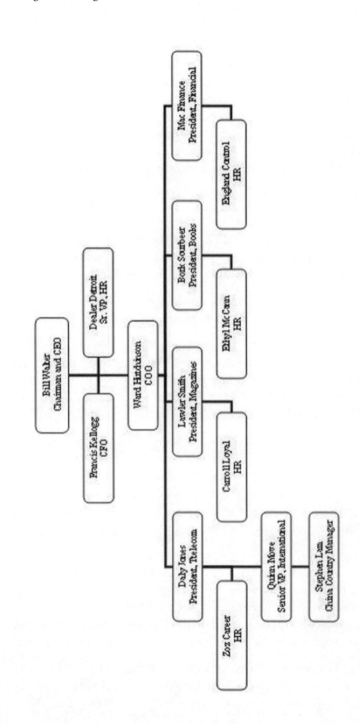

Bork Sourbeer, the Books President, was a legacy employee who pursued acquisitions in direct mailing business to supplement growth in the book printing business.

Mac Finance, the Financial President, focused on proprietary pharmaceutical and capital market printing requirements, including a high security internet space to exchange drafts of documents such as prospecti in order to secure financial printing customers.

### *Hiring of Mark Chen*

Mark Chen was a schoolmate of Bill with a proven record of success developing and managing businesses in Asia, including profitable startup operations in China. An Asian American executive with impeccable credentials and a successful career track record turning investments into profitable businesses, he seemed an ideal candidate to help Bill achieve his vision. After an initial meeting, an interview was setup with Ward Hutchinson and Daly Jones who supported the hiring of Mark.

Since each segment President was measured on the profitability of their respective segment, special incentives had to be developed to hire Mark and encourage growth in multimedia business and/or overseas expansion. Daly Jones proposed a special program where Mark would be exposed to the entire ABC Company over a two year period, before deciding if the internet space or Asian expansion would be the right career path for Mark. From the organization structure, it was logical to have Mark report to the Senior Vice President of International Operations Quinn Move because Mark can learn printing and international operations from Quinn. Mark was privately informed that he would replace Quinn as soon as he was ready. Despite negative feedback regarding the culture of this organization, Mark took the position thinking it was a win-win solution to transform corporate culture mandated from the top of the organization.

### *Mark Chen's Orientation*

Zoz Career, the Human Resource Specialist who did not participate in the hiring of Mark, was not aware that Mark was hired as an executive higher in rank than the China Country Manager, and treated Mark as a new college graduate. Quinn Move did not intervene until Zoz already spent substantial effort assembling a two-year program for Mark. During orientation, Zoz welcomed Mark and said, "I am glad you are here, because Stephen Lam (China Country Manager and not a US citizen) had to be controlled."

When Quinn informed Zoz that Mark was already a senior executive, Zoz pointed out to the administrative staff in front of Mark that Mark demanded special treatment because he was a high ranking employee. She apologized profusely to Mark, and restructured the entire orientation program and the two-year development program that included both Internet space and printing operational assignments. She also confided in Mark that she was looking forward to an international career with ABC.

### *Mark Chen's Career Path*

After a one month orientation to visit different facilities, Mark was assigned to the second largest printing facility in North America, with 32 web presses and over 1,000 employees in 1 million square foot of space. Again, the Human Resource specialist of the plant, Cheryl Sharp, was not aware of Mark's status, and assigned a college entry level position to Mark. When this was reported to Quinn, Mark was assigned Senior Manager of Manufacturing Services, overseeing the maintenance and support of the printing operations, and became part of the Plant Manager staff. As this was the period when Y2K virus was a major concern, Information Technology and Y2K responsibilities were assigned to Mark as well. In addition, Daly Jones added the responsibility of negotiating Internet investments to Mark, managed out of corporate headquarters, and outside the responsibility of the Plant Manager who demanded 24-hour service from his staff.

After an uneventful Y2K, Mark made a presentation on the Internet investment plan to Bill Walter and Ward Hutchinson which was approved for execution. The subsequent negotiations made it difficult for Mark to continue in the Plant Manager's staff. Instead of a 9-month assignment described in the two-year development program, the printing assignment ended after four months on a part time basis.

As Mark began his assignment to bring content to the Internet, he traveled extensively to visit the content owners–the publishers, for approval to use the electronic content beyond printing. Each content owner must see value for this additional use of the content before permission can be given. During this time frame, Mark successfully negotiated with another Internet startup company, along with key system integrators such as IBM and Motorola, to deliver yellow page content in both Shanghai and Beijing, the first time such electronic content can be searched using cellular phones anywhere in China.

Three months later, Stephen Lam, the China Country Manager, resigned after three years on the job due to personal reasons. The resignation was immediately accepted, and Mark was offered the position of President of Asia, still reporting to Quinn Move. Mark suggested that Quinn Move may be a better candidate, but it was not approved. Instead, Quinn assembled a very attractive compensation package for Mark, and Daly Jones strongly encouraged Mark to take the position, indicating support by Ward Hutchinson and Bill Walter. Bill Walter directly communicated to Mark, supporting Mark as the representative to drive growth in Asia for ABC. Reluctantly, Mark moved his family overseas after completing the first internet investment. The two year program was deemed complete within eight months.

### *Ground Truth Overseas*

Upon arrival in Asia, Mark learned that the facility was unprofitable, even with fully depreciated equipment. With less than 10% of the web presses, the workforce was more than half the size of the second largest printing facility in North America. Very few of the workforce were familiar with basic quality control, such as Statistical Process Control, and corruption was rampant. Mark had to commute five hours each day to the factory, sometimes even sleeping at the facility. Through his network, Mark hired one of the most prominent local statisticians in China to conduct training for the entire workforce, and began to identify competent staff to automate Pre-Media operations.

With the renewed emphasis on Pre-Media operations, combined with the delivery of yellow page electronic content to cellular phones, ABC achieved "High Technology Enterprise" designation from the Chinese government. This translated into an estimated US$20 million of tax savings if the facility continued to turn a profit.

Quinn was focused on his requirements as Mark's supervisor, and worked directly with a consultant on plans to directly negotiate with a Chinese partner on a second JV. He demanded detailed productivity improvement plans, and performance metrics information from Mark on a continuing basis, directed an Indian expatriate and an American expatriate to duplicate the quality training in English, did not support the return of a capable Pre-Media Manager after giving him a temporary assignment in the US, and refused to confirm his consent in writing to correct a fire code violation.

The growing number of issues reached a cracking point when Quinn sponsored an additional training program for the top managers in China without making the agenda available to Mark. The training session, conducted by an American expatriate based in Beijing and facilitated by Mark, was going well until Quinn Move changed the agenda by dictating performance expectations. The employees were confused and believed training was unnecessary if the performance expectations were dictated. The American trainer was upset and clearly communicated to Quinn Move in front of Mark and others that Quinn Move was clearly destroying the credibility with his blatant disrespect of Mark.

Mark caught up with the second JV investment when he was asked to present the investment to the ABC Executive Committee. Quinn insisted that Mark make the presentation because Mark was responsible for the project. Upon review of the presentation, Mark believed that the proposed investment was based on unrealistic market projections from the consultant. Mark obtained agreement from Quinn that the consultant would discuss the market projections during the presentation. The investment was approved for execution.

Mark was determined to communicate his unsustainable work environment in China. However, he learned that Daly Jones and Bill Walter believed they knew what's going on in Asia, so there was no need for additional meetings.

Mark left ABC soon afterwards.

*People will get what they deserve in the long run.*

*—Karma*

# Case #5 Epilogue

# ABC Printing Company

<u>Note</u>

ABC has a tremendous advantage with an existing 90+% ownership of the existing facility that no other foreign entity can duplicate in this industry until after 2005, when China committed to opening the market under the new WTO rules. The Chinese partner was a powerful local government official who regularly attended Central Government meetings in Beijing. There were personality issues between the Chinese partner and an ABC executive that created difficult Board meetings. Since the existing JV has not demonstrated a profit motive, it would be more difficult to demonstrate a profit motive in the second JV with minority ownership. The negative impact on shareholder value, however, may be invisible since it is not clear if the minority ownership of the second JV would be consolidated.

ABC had a window of opportunity to sustain its competitive advantage by building quality, service, and new technology especially in Pre-Media to support growth and profit in China. The difficulty was managing Quinn Move, a Caucasian with 30+year work experience in ABC who wanted to be an expatriate in Hong Kong.

Bill Walter must establish a process for succession planning plus objective channels of communication in order to protect the company and its investments. He reaffirmed his commitment to pursuing the "Ground Truth" during this visit to China. He knew that ABC lost at least five years of progress when Quinn Move moved to Asia and added expatriate staff-reverting back to the original structure before the operations were profitable. The penalties to the company included:

- Higher cost structure with more expatriate staff under Quinn.
- Lower revenue/profit due to less than committed sales team.
- Losing US$25 million new facility investment when the market projections to justify the investment may not be realizable.
- Lower brand value in the marketplace and thereafter lower shareholder value.
- Poor reputation and lower employee loyalty=lower quality and higher turnover.

The Ground Truth, as he learned:

Quinn Move told Mark Chen he would like to retire in the Far East and confused Mark by not confirming his interest in moving to Asia when Mark recommended Quinn for the Asia position. When Ward Hutchinson resigned, Daly Jones focused on his corporate responsibilities and was promoted to a corporate position before he left the company.

Three communications paths available to Mark Chen were controlled by Quinn Move: Operations Management, Human Resources, and New Business Development.

Quinn Move insisted on detailed data from operations management that consumed Mark's time and effort. Hundreds of pages of productivity improvement activities must be generated, summarized, and presented.

By driving the China top management training, Quinn Move controlled communications with Human Resources. It did not matter that the external trainer vehemently objected to Quinn Move's intervention during the training. The confusion destroyed the value of training. Quinn leveraged this confusion to strengthen his position as Mark's successor.

New Business Development required justification for new investments. Investments must be justified by a business plan with market projections. Printing requires substantial capital investment up front, before the customers fill the web presses and deliver profit. The consultant responsible for the market projections revealed that the market projection was driven by Quinn Move to justify the investment, and the related market share capture may be unrealistic. The consultant believed that the entire team will be replaced by the time the projected market must become revenue and profit for the company, therefore Mark should not interfere with the approval process.

Quinn Move gave Mark Chen a lucrative compensation package and created an environment so he can be Mark's successor. He succeeded.

# Appendix

# Talking point starters

The "talking point starters" collected below will help you engage your Chinese counterparts. As illustrated in the "Engaging your counterpart" section, you need to put these "starters" in the proper context as you engage your Chinese counterparts. Based on meetings during my 8 years in China, this is a cursory overview of some intricate historical events and developments that have influenced China's relationship with the West.

Study these "starters" to help you develop your own set of relevant "talking points."

*Early Chinese History*

Daniel Quinn's book *Ishmael* (Bantam Books, 1992) describes the agricultural revolution and may serve as a departure point.

**Throughout human history, the ability to "do" has been driven by the ability to "command"**–resources, money and people. As we created tools to hunt better, we mimicked "hunter" animals until we learned to "command the earth" via agriculture. As we produced more food, we increased our population. Then our need to support our own "animals" drove us into conflict with competitors and, eventually, spawned regional wars and global empires.

In recent history, the British created one model for establishing an empire: Colonize foreign lands to command new resources. China, meanwhile, worked on another: Conquer neighboring territories to bring northern Asian neighbors under its influence. Internally, the Chinese also developed ways to segregate their society into laborers, intellectuals, warriors, and administrators to command its own resources.

**Note**

Though trade between peoples and countries has flourished from the earliest points in history, generally the world has existed as a set of relatively isolated regions ("spheres of influence") with ethnic identities, religious beliefs and social customs developing in geographical "pockets." Values and cultural practices that evolved reflected the uniqueness of each region. Conflicts were relatively small in scale and localized. While the pursuit of commerce did introduce some religious and cultural influences to different parts of the world, seldom did the societies overlap.

The British-led drive for finding new resources in new territories created the most recent round of colonization (two centuries ago). That brought the British to India, and helped "open" up China. The rest, as the saying goes, "is history."

### Values and Religion

Students of religion understand the evolution of value systems. That evolution is important to your understanding of the Chinese.

The world's major religions—Judaism, Christianity, Islam, Hinduism and Buddhism—were dominant forces that shaped the culture and value systems in their own regions (or "spheres of influence"). Together, 4.5 billion of the world's 6 billion population[2] follow these religions today.

Some religions found their way into China through missionary work and migration, with Buddhism having the greatest impact. To this day, Chinese values, social customs and cultural practices reflect the teachings of Buddhism, but also of Confucianism and Daoism, the belief systems of two secular philosopher-educators from two millennia ago. While not officially endorsed by the Chinese government, all three have gained religion-like adherents and related practices.

### Chinese Innovation

While Western European countries are widely credited with their own contributions to the global innovation, China's wonderfully rich history of innovation has been less well-known because of its inward-focused civilization for many centuries. In the earliest of time, Chinese innovation was driven by practicality and became the primary force behind productivity in its class-based society.

The catalog of Chinese innovation and invention is extensive: Compass, gunpowder, dams, paper, printing, and fireworks, etc. (This list can be extended considerably, and some research will prove fruitful.)

### Early Trade

More than a thousand years ago, Chinese trade was dominated by the interior province of Anhui, as represented in the adage, "Transactions aren't complete without a merchant from Anhui." Trade took some early Chinese merchants beyond their shores to Southeast Asia, India and the Middle East. While opinions differ, some Chinese hold the beliefs that 1) Chinese traders reached American shores before Christopher Columbus and 2) Native Americans were Asians who had traveled to the North American continent via Alaska's Bering Strait.

Trade in the West, on the other hand, was often "supported" with "gunboat diplomacy"–which may help explain why Western traders were more successful at penetrating their commercial "targets" so thoroughly. And because the Industrial Revolution had its birth in the West, it was Western societies that harnessed machinery to overhaul and supplement their productivity of their workforce to achieve impressive economic development and growth.

### War in the 20th century

As populations increased, the world became smaller and our differences created more conflicts. Sometimes we fought over resources, sometimes over values. In the 20th century, two tragedies of World War II have left long-term scars on the histories of China and Japan:

- An estimated 20-25 million Chinese died during the various phases of the conflict, including at least 18 million civilians.

- In the effort to end that war, the US dropped two atomic bombs in Japan, killing an estimated 200,000 people, and impacting the lives of millions more.

### Recent Chinese History

Beginning in the early 1800's, foreigners (representing the US, Britain, Germany, France, Russia, Japan, Spain, and Italy) entered China with gunboats for trade, often showing little respect for the people with whom they conducted business. One tragic consequence was the introduction of opium mostly by the British in the early 19th century which had a devastating effect on large portions of the population coaxed into its addictive use.

Circa World War II, there were signs in Shanghai's Bund area park that warned "Dogs and Chinese not allowed." (If you are a US citizen, picture a parallel situation in New York City's Central Park, with signs saying "Dogs and US Citizens not allowed" and you might better relate what this means.) These acts of condescension spawned the impression that "foreign devils" aren't trustworthy. That perception is still prevalent today: Many of the problems foreign businesses find in China are rooted in these suspicions, which are also a likely factor in the Chinese's slow progress in protecting foreign intellectual property rights.

Recent xenophobia is an extreme form of these suspicions, and was the policy approach of the Communist government after founding the People's Republic of China in 1949. Between 1949 and 1978, China turned inward to concentrate on feeding its own population. People were mobilized to work in the farms and countryside. To this day, 65% of the 1.3 billion Chinese work in agriculture and related areas.

From 30 years of self-imposed isolation, including 10 years of the infamous Cultural Revolution, China fell behind the global trading community in both economic and technological advances. It was Deng Xiaoping who led China's reengagement with the world in 1978. But even as it opened its doors to foreign nations, China was careful about selecting trade partners that respected its sovereignty and initially limited the areas in which foreigners could do business. The mistrust and suspicion of foreigners developed over many years were still factors that influenced the slow pace with which China's doors have been reopened.

The most recent transition of power under Communist China occurred in 2003 when Hu Jintao became China's new President. Interestingly, Hu is a native of Anhui Province, where trade was once dominant over 1,000 years ago. It's a good omen for China's bright future.

## US History and Chinese Immigration

The relationship between the United States and China has been shaped by many of the developments of recent centuries. As a new country that promised a better life and new opportunities, the US attracted many immigrants from China.

Once here, however, the Chinese discovered great disappointment. The lives they envisioned–the kind of work they could pursue and where they could live–were severely limited. Yet these early immigrants persevered and, along with African-Americans and other minorities, formed a formidable labor force that supported industrial and technological advances that helped the US modernize. These included working on the transcontinental railroad and in the fisheries, as well as in manufacturing and other industries. But all this was not without struggle and controversy. Perceived as a threat to the established unionized labor force, the Chinese were discriminated against with the passage of the Chinese Exclusion Act of 1882, a law that was contrary to the spirit of the Emancipation Proclamation of 1863 and in violation of the Burlingame Treaty of 1868.[52] This discrimination against its US-based citizens helped contribute to the negative perceptions that Chinese have of all foreigners.

It was not until 1943 that Congress repealed the Chinese Exclusion Act, just as China became an ally in World War II. Since then, more Chinese immigrants have been able to make their homes in the US and their children and grandchildren have been assimilated into the American society. The US has had a history of discrimination against minorities, but to its credit, the nation has also come to terms with its past by enacting legislation to undo much of those prejudices, such as the 19th Amendment to the US Constitution on women's suffrage in 1920 and the Civil Rights Act of 1964.

These actions have not entirely done away with prejudicial and discriminatory attitudes in the American society. But as a global leader, the US continues to initiate and recognize diversity, and to encourage fairer treatment of all citizens. **For the most part, Americans are viewed favorably by the Chinese today** and the Chinese do appreciate the openness and straight forward way in which they are often treated by their American counterparts in business, academia and government.

*Mass communications*

One of the great achievements of the 20th century was growing capacity to communicate with large audiences. Early on, radio and the telegraph formed the infrastructure for communicating with a global audience. By 2001, communications advances are expanding our access to information through broadband multi-media.

China Telecom, the dominant carrier in China, operates the second-largest SDH (Synchronous Digital Hierarchy) network in the world, and China is second only to the US in its Dense Wave Division Multiplexing (DWDM) implementation (see Genteli Telecom–*Case #4*). When satellite communications are introduced, there will be another major influx of information technology advancement.

Yet even in this fast paced information age, the Chinese still resort to the traditional practice of taking time to identify trustworthy business partners. The key is, once you establish trust–however long it takes–the Chinese become willing partners and help drive your success.

*Economic Union and WTO*

We are merging together as a global economic community. Even though pockets of isolations still exist, they are few in number and exert less and less influence. The United Nations provides a forum for dialogue among nations. There are many cross border alliances, the most conspicuous of which are trading blocs. Examples: The Organization of Petroleum Exporting Countries (OPEC), which demonstrated its economic power in 1973, and again in 1978 (the so-called "oil shocks"). Europe merged as a single European Union (EU) in 1991. Other multi-nation trading blocs include the North American Free Trade Area (NAFTA), Association of Southeastern Asian Nations (ASEAN), and Asian Pacific Economic Community (APEC).

In 1995, the World Trade Organization (WTO), whose predecessor was the General Agreement on Tariffs and Trade (GATT), was established after the Uruguay round of negotiations.[53] As of 2003, 145 nations are now committed to international rules of commerce under the WTO. The WTO is the main global forum for dialogue on trade issues, similar to the United Nations on security and related issues. One of the greatest values of the WTO is that it establishes standards for global trade practices through agreements ratified by member countries. Producers of goods and services, and importers and exporters rely on these standards of global trade to conduct their business.

Until 2001, China was a trading nation, but not a WTO member. The US had kept China in a trading category similar to Cuba and Libya, which required annual government approvals to gain "Most Favored Nation" trade status. Of the world's 6 billion people, over half are in Asia, and 1.3 billion are in China. With China excluded as a member, the WTO could not credibly claim to represent the global community. China's accession to the WTO in 2001 was, therefore, a major step for China and for world trade. The significance of this was that 20% of the world's population, represented by one country, committed to abiding by the rules of international trade.

*Summary*

Buyers and sellers alike win with successful trading. As often touted by the Chinese, the US offers advanced technologies, workforce diversity and management know-how while China offers low cost labor and a vast consumer market. From China's perspective, there are many win-win opportunities in this partnership scenario.

**Note**

As a business executive considering the lure of a growing and lucrative marketplace in China, you will face many challenges. Some will seem familiar if you're a veteran of other international markets, and some will definitely be unique. Understanding the differences and being prepared to deal with these challenges by recruiting and nurturing those who will best represent you and work for you, will go a long way to helping you succeed and be profitable in this vast country of opportunities.

# Footnotes

## Dedication

[1] There are many articles on SARS. The official website from Center for Disease Control and Prevention is: http://www.cdc.gov/ncidod/sars/. Typical stories includes: "WHO sees SARS slowing but new cases reported," by Tan Ee Lyn, Reuters (via Yahoo News), April 7, 2003. The reported cases were approaching 10,000 with 8% mortality at press time. The website with the official information is: http://www.who.int/csr/sarscountry/en/. According to Stanford University's website: www.stanford.edu/group/virus/uda/ , the world's most devastating epidemic was the Spanish flu of 1918-1919 when 20-40 million people died around the world, after infecting 20% of the world's population.

## Snapshot of China's Place in Our World

[2] Breakdown of religions of the world by population in 2000:

| | | |
|---|---|---|
| Muslim | 1.28 billion | (mostly, Middle East, Indonesia) |
| Buddhism | 0.40 billion | (mostly China, India, Thailand) |
| Judaism | 0.01 billion | (mostly Israel) |
| Christians | 1.03 billion | (mostly Americas and Europe) |
| Catholics | 0.94 billion | (mostly Americas and Europe) |
| Hindu | 0.82 billion | (mostly India) |
| No religion | 0.94 billion | |
| Chinese | 0.39 billion | |
| Tradit. Ethnic | 0.18 billion | |
| Sikhs | 0.02 billion | |
| Others | 0.06 billion | |
| Total | 6.07 billion | (world population growing at 1.39%/year) |

Source: Operation World Website, January 7, 2003, website address: http://www.gmi.org/ow/region/wor/owtext.html#ppl

Author's note: Chinese, per se, is not a religion. The Chinese never established its own religion to reflect their values in more than 5,000 years of sovereign existence. (See *Talking point starters* in *Appendix*).

[3] Geographically, the 2002 population data by Continent (in millions), based on http://www.prb.org/pdf/WorldPopulationDS02_Eng.pdf

| | |
|---|---|
| China | 1,281 |
| Asia (other than China) | 2,485 |
| North America | 319 |
| Latin America & Caribbean | 531 |
| Oceana | 32 |
| Europe | 728 |
| Africa | 840 |
| Total | 6,215 |

[4] Greater China has US$365.1 billion foreign reserves or US$24 billion more than Japan in 2000. The detailed Foreign Currency Reserves Ranking follows:

| Country | US$ billion | As at end of |
|---|---|---|
| (1) Japan | 341.1 | May 2000 |
| (2) China | 156.8 | Mar 2000 |
| (3) Taiwan | 113.1 | May 2000 |
| (4) Hong Kong | 95.2 | May 2000 |
| (5) Germany | 87.0 | Apr 2000 |
| (6) Korea | 86.8 | May 2000 |
| (7) Singapore | 75.4 | Apr 2000 |
| (8) US | 67.2 | May 2000 |
| (9) France | 65.3 | Apr 2000 |
| (10) Italy | 46.6 | Apr 2000 |

Sources: HKMA, Reuters, Deutsche Bundesbank, Monetary Authority of Singapore, US Department of Treasury, Bank of Italy.

[5] The Global GDP on PPP Basis was US$38.8 trillion in 2000. (Source: Background notes, Indian Petrochem 2002, http://www.eliteconferences.com/bgnotes.htm). The distribution of World GDP on PPP Basis for the top 17 countries for 2000 was as follows:

| Country | % of World GDP |
|---|---|
| United States | 22.0% |
| China | 11.5% |
| Japan | 7.3% |
| India | 4.6% |
| Germany | 4.5% |
| France | 3.2% |
| United Kingdom | 3.1% |
| Italy | 3.1% |
| Brazil | 2.7% |
| Russia | 2.5% |
| Canada | 1.9% |
| Mexico | 1.9% |
| Spain | 1.7% |
| South Korea | 1.7% |
| Indonesia | 1.5% |
| Australia | 1.1% |
| Taiwan | 1.0% |
| Total of 17 countries: | 75.3% |

Source: World Economic News, quoting IMF's World Economic Outlook, October 2001.
(http://www.worldgameofeconomics.com/GlobalEconomy_2001.html)

Adding US, Germany, France, UK, Italy, Spain and Australia equals 38.7% of the US$38.8 trillion Global GDP of US$15 trillion. Selecting China and Taiwan equals 12.5% or US$5 trillion.

## Chapter 1

[6] There are 24 million businesses in the US that files income tax returns (5 million corporations, 2 million partnerships/LLCs, 17 million sole proprietorships), according to the statistical information from bizstats.com, edited by Patrick O-Rourke, Washington, DC, 2003. There are 16 million European enterprises equally divided among Microenterprises, Small and Medium Enterprises, and Large Enterprises, according to the European Union "European Industrial Strategy", Agenda 2000 package of proposals. This is also quoted in UNICE's Council of Presidents meetings in Helsinki on December 3, 1999. There are 2 million businesses in Australia, including 1.4 million non-employing entities (which roughly translate into sole proprietorships).

[7] Foreign Direct Investment in China gradually increased to US$40 billion per year in the 1990s, and jumped to US$50 billion actual investment and US$70 billion contracted investment in 2002, possibly exceeding FDI of the US for the first time, and become the world's largest FDI recipient. "China to Draw US$50 billion FDI, to be World #1 Recipient", Peoples' Daily, December 5, 2002.

[8] "International Comparisons of PPP based economy", IMF 1993 data, Professor Vladimir Treml, THE ECONOMIST October 1, 1994,

[9] http://www.macrochina.com.cn/english/index/china/imagse/china_gnp.jpg, 1/12/2003.

[10] There are many quotes in the media regarding 21st century high growth in Asia Pacific. For example: Secretary of State Colin Powell June 10th, 2002 address to Asia Society: "I have no doubt that Asia's great transformation…will only accelerate in this new century…I see in Asia…a growing awareness that the 21st century holds extraordinary opportunities…". See also "President's visit: Hallmark in Sino-Indian Ties", by Darshan Singh, http://www.dailyexcelsior.com/00july04/edit.htm

[11] "In China, Building Worries" by Peter Goodman, The Washington Post, March 5, 2003

[12] Sue Herrera, CNBC Special Report on China, December 25, 2002

[13] Sue Herrera, CNBC Special Report on China, December 25, 2002

[14] Shanghai Debuts Futuristic Rail System, by Martin Fackler, AP Writer, 12/31/2002.

[15] "China's Manned Space Flight Ever Nearer", Peoples' Daily Newspaper Website Article, January 9, 2003

[16] Haier is a trademark of the Haier Company, Qingdao, Shandong, China.

[17] "The well heeled upstart on Cisco's tail", by Bruce Einhorn in Shenzhen, Ben Elgin in San Mateo, California, and Andy Reinhardt in Paris, page 91, Business Week, October 28, 2002

[18] Sue Herrera, CNBC Special Report on China, December 25, 2002

[19] Beta is a measure of risk under the capital asset pricing model commonly used in the investment banking community. There are many books on this topic. For example: "Investments", 4th Edition, by Zvi Bodie, Alex Kane, Alan Marcus, Irwin McGraw-Hill Publications, 2001

[20] There are two books by the same authors on core competencies: "The Core Competence of the Corporation", by CK Prahalad & Gary Hamel, Harvard Business Review, 68(3), p. 79-91, May, 1990 and "Competing for the future" by CK Prahalad and Gary Hamel, Harvard Business School Press, 1996

[21] An estimate of the cost of overseas assignments and traveling for US, Australian and European businesses in Greater China is between US$30-50 billion dollars per year (100,000 to 200,000 expatriate families at US$200,000-500,000 per family), based on discussions with executive search firms in China and Hong Kong as well as an informal survey conducted by Wu & Associates LLC.

[22] "The company defines diversity as competitive advantage", AlliedSignal Engineering Materials newsletter "Matters", November 1994

[23] For example, new regulations on trademarks have been implemented with significant improvements over previous rules in order to bring the Trademark Law's subsidiary legislation into line with the amended Trademark Law and WTO requirements. Procedures at the Trademark Office have been streamlined, greater protection of well-known trademarks is available and fines that may be imposed against infringers have been increased. "The Implementing Regulations for the Trademark Law of the Peoples' Republic of China", promulgated by the State Council on August 3rd, 2002, and came into force on September 15, 2002. For certain elements of intellectual property, Hong Kong already has one of the most stringent intellectual properties laws and regulations in place. A good source of information is the e-newsletter distributed by Angela Wong & Co. in Hong Kong. Email: lawyers@angelawangco.com.

## Chapter 2

[24] A fictional account of seeking the weakest point in a process to support continuous improvement is illustrated in the book "The Goal", by Eliyahu M. Goldratt and Jeff Cox, North River Press Publishing Corporation, 2nd Revised Edition, May 1992

[25] "Inside Chinese Business: A Guide for Managers Worldwide", by Ming-Jer Chen, Boston: Harvard Business School Press, 2001

[26] "Doing Business in China", by Time Ambler and Morgen Witzel, New York: Routledge, 2000

[27] A good reference for McDonald's early experience is "Golden Arches East–McDonald's in East Asia", by James Watson, Stanford Press, 1997

## Chapter 3

[28] "Chinese Business Etiquette: A Guide to Protocol, Manners, and Culture in the People's Republic of China", By Scott D. Seligman, Warner Books, 1999

[29] "Culture Shock Inventory" is a psychological test originally developed by WJ Reddin with 648 responses and expanded non-commercially by Wu & Associates LLC. Contact the author with questions at dswu@alumni.princeton.edu.

## Chapter 4

[30] The general expatriate package information was reviewed by China Team International, an executive search group based in Shanghai, China. Annual salary surveys and related information are available through AmCham or consulting firms such as Mercer.

## Chapter 5

[31] The seven AmChams in China are located in Chengdu, Guangdong, Shanghai, Beijing, Tianjin, Hong Kong, and Taipei.

[32] Some typical publications are "IP Protection in China–Practical Strategies", Second Edition, By Toby Curthoys, Managing Editor, Asia Law and Practice Publishing Ltd., Euromoney Publications, 1998.

33 "Brands–the new wealth creators", edited by Susannah Hart and John Murphy, Interbrand, MacMillan Press, Ltd, 1998

34 18,000 Jews fled Germany, Austria, and Poland and arrived in Shanghai between 1938-1939, after 30,000 Jews were arrested on November 9, 1938 (also known as "crystal night") and sent to concentration camps in Dachau and Buchenwald at the beginning of the Holocaust. "Jews recall life in Shanghai 50 years after fleeing Nazis", by Mary Sedor, AP Writer, story published in The Miami Herald, Sunday, October 16, 1988, Page 9A.

## Section III

35 The concept of formal and informal workplace networks are also discussed in Diversity Training Seminars in the US (e.g. courses such as Consulting Pairs, and Managing Personnel Diversity, offered by Pope & Associates in Cincinnati). Another source is DiversityUniversity.com, an eLearning environment for courses in "Joining Up."

36 Character First! Training Institute is a US based non-profit organization to promote character development in individuals from all walks of life. The premise is character transcends race, religion, education, position, gender, and personality. The website is: www.characterfirst.org. Training is available in both China and the US.

37 "Best Employers China" segment of Best Employers of Asia survey conducted in 2001 by Hewitt Associates. The release date for the 2003 joint Harvard Business Review China and Hewitt Associates study is April, 2003. See www.bestemployersasia.com. The 2001 survey consisted of 95,000 employees in 355 companies and 26 industries across 10 regions in Asia, of which 13,133 employees in 51 companies in 19 industries participated in China. The scope will be broader in the 2003 survey.

38 The American Motors Corp. Chinese investment in Jeep manufacturing is well documented in "Beijing Jeep: A Case Study of Western Business in China", by Jim Mann, Westview Press, 1997

39 "China Business: The Rules of the Game" by Carolyn Blackman, New South Wales, Australia: Allen & Unwin, 2000

40 "The 100 Best Companies to Work For", the 2000 survey by Levering and Moskowitz, Fortune, January 10, 2001, as presented by Hewitt Associates "Best Employers China" presentation, August 2002. The 3-year, 5-year, and 10-year

returns for Best Companies were 37%, 34%, and 21%, compared to the Standard & Poor's 500 companies composite return of 25%, 25%, and 17%, respectively.

[41] "Are the 100 Best Better? An Empirical Investigation of the Relationship between being a Best Employer and Firm Performance", by Gerhart, Fulmer, Scott, Vanderbilt University and Hewitt Associates, as presented by Hewitt Associates "Best Employers China" presentation, August 2002. The voluntary turnover and (employment) applications per employee for the top 25 companies were 7.6% and 3.5, compared to the rest of the companies in the empirical investigation at 11.8%, and 2.6, respectively.

## Chapter 6

[42] "Execution: The Discipline of Getting Things Done", by Lawrence A Bossidy and Ram Charan, Crown Business, June 11, 2002

[43] Since "home" for Taiwan and Hong Kong expatriates is not your home office, some of the discussions on expatriates' culture do not apply. We discuss them separately in *Chapter 8*. Suffice it say that expatriates from regional offices and your "home base" should emulate their own home office whenever possible.

[44] This example may not be well received by expert historians. In the business world, the nepotism was also observed in many companies. One example is Wang Lab in the US when An Wang gave management of his company to his son Frederick Wang.

## Chapter 7

[45] "High Tech in China: Is it a threat to Silicon Valley", by Bruce Einhorn, Ben Elgin and Andy Reinhardt, Business Week, McGraw Hill Publications, October 28, 2002

[46] "China ranked fourth in Asia in average TOEFL scores", People's Daily online, February 5, 2000, http://fpeng.peopledaily.com.cn/200002/05/eng20000205U100.html.

[47] "China's one child policy: Anomaly or necessity?" by Xin Zuo, Stockholm School of Economics & EIJS, 1997

## Chapter 8

48 "China's population growth and its economic boom," by A. A. Bennet, Iowa State University, website address: http://www.meteor.iastate.edu/gcp/energy/china.html. This is a course description using data from China through 1995.

49 "The Hong Kong Experiment", by Milton Friedman (Nobel Laureate Economist), Hoover Digest, #3, 1998

## Chapter 9

50 Data from China Council for Promotion of International Trade and China Chamber of International Commerce. Non-Chinese enterprises include those funded by "foreign companies" as well as Hong Kong, Taiwan, and Macau invested companies. The data used is for the year 2000, with comparative information for 1999 to calculate growth rates. This data can be viewed from the website address: www.ccpit.org

51 "The 100 Best Companies to Work for in America (Serial)", by Robert Levering and Milton Moskowitz, Plume Publishing, 1994. This survey has been updated through Fortune Magazine on an annual basis. See www.fortune.com/fortune/bestcompanies.

## Appendix: Talking point starters

52The US signed The Burlingame Treaty of 1868 which promised never to exclude Chinese immigration. "The Heathen Chinee–A study of American Attitudes toward China, 1890-1905", by Robert McClellan, Ohio State University Press, 1971. For a current discussion on Chinese Americans, Bill Moyers' PBS Special "Becoming Americans" aired in March 2003. See: http://www.pbs.org/becomingamerican/.

53 "The WTO", www.wto.org/english/thewto_e/thewto_e.htm. The number of countries is from http://www.countrywatch.com/@School/number_countries.htm. 145 countries are WTO members out of a total of 192 countries in the world (March, 2003).

# Index

*Life is a succession of lessons*
*which must be lived to be understood.*

*—Helen Keller*

# About the Author

David S. Wu is an avid fan of continuous improvement who loves to share his experiences in the spirit of mutual learning. Readers are encouraged to contact him at dswu@alumni.princeton.edu.

He has worked effectively among many cultures including Caucasian, African-American, Asian-American, and Asian. After spending 8 years stationed overseas managing businesses in Asia for several Fortune 500 companies, he returned to McLean, Virginia to devote time to serving as President of Wu & Associates LLC. TIME magazine wrote an article on David's return in 2002, and the concept of writing a book emerged. He is committed to help build and sustain winning cultures for businesses worldwide. As Senior Consultant to China Team International, an executive search firm based in Greater China and a member of the Cornerstone Group, he helps companies identify candidates for China operations. As Project Consultant for Pope & Associates, he presents diversity workshops that can drive higher profitability performance in global organizations.

David has over 20 years working experience, and was among the highest ranking Asian American in his company for 14 of those years. Since 1994, he traveled extensively throughout US and Asia to deliver US$40 million operating profit and US$300 million sales. His assignments included Regional Manager of Greater China for Tyco Fire & Security, VP and COO of Teligent-Hong Kong, President of R. R. Donnelley Far East, Managing Director of Danaher Instrument and Control Group in China, and President and CFO of Honeywell-China Eastern Airlines JV where he negotiated the only profitable investment for AlliedSignal in China before the Honeywell acquisition.

Prior to working overseas, he worked for AlliedSignal (now Honeywell) soon after Larry Bossidy left GE to become Chairman and CEO of AlliedSignal in 1991. By examining the cost structure of all businesses, he was responsible for the first corporate wide measurement of Productivity in the 1992 Annual Report based on the GE methodology. He actively participated in teams to drive new businesses such as Optical Polymers for Flat Panel Displays, and coordinated the Asian Roundtable to develop growth strategies for Asia that led to the hiring of the first employees in Asia for the Engineered Materials Sector of AlliedSignal. It was his role as Director of Asian Business Development for Aerospace Equipment Systems and Director of China Programs for Aircraft Landing Systems that guided him to identify China Eastern Airlines as an attractive partner in China. He negotiated the joint venture from conception to business license in one year.

David was attracted to Honeywell (AlliedSignal) from BFGoodrich where, as Manager of Finance at Corporate Headquarters, he prepared business plans for a new venture investment in stereolithography. He started in BFGoodrich as Assistant Controller of Finance and Analysis in the Aerospace Division, after working for the Helicopters Division of Boeing where he established the Strategic Planning department, describing the global market and strategies to become the world's largest rotorcraft manufacturer. Boeing Helicopters is the world's largest Rotorcraft manufacturer today.

David has been a Board member or Advisor to numerous technology and/or Internet companies. He has published and presented on numerous technical and business topics ranging from handling nuclear power plant issues to delivering Yellow Pages content to cellular phones in Shanghai and Beijing. His credentials include Certified Public Accountant, Certified Management Accountant, Professional Engineer-In-Training, Wharton MBA, University of Pennsylvania

MSE, and Princeton BSE where he has been active in Asian Alumni of Princeton and the Princeton Alumni Schools Committee. He completed the Professional Accounting Program of Kellogg School as an Arthur Young (now Ernst & Young) Fellow, Managerial Issues in Global Enterprise Program of the Thunderbird School as an AlliedSignal (now Honeywell) executive, and Leadership at the Peak Program at the Center for Creative Leadership as a R. R. Donnelley executive.

He grew up in Washington DC where he attended DC Public Schools as a scholar athlete in Football, Soccer, and Track and has coached youth soccer in both US and China. His interest in business was piqued while working for The Evening Star Newspaper Company, an organization that selected him as one of its Best Newspaper Carriers in Metropolitan DC in 1972, 1973, and 1974.

# About the Editor

Lee Dudka, a business writer and strategist for Fortune 500 drug and technology companies, has begun his second quarter-century as a consultant to individuals and teams. He coaches senior executives (foreign and American) in extended programs throughout the United States and has done so for 19 years.

His specialty: Coaching on "next-step action pointers" for people and organizations looking for better strategy "roadmaps," improved operations or clearer messages. He writes and edits books; develops teams; creates executive speeches. He consults regularly for Bristol-Myers Squibb, Johnson & Johnson, Pharmacia, Marriott, CACI, Telos, federal and local government, major universities (Princeton, Rutgers, Tufts) and non-profits.

胡氏企業

*That which is good is never finished.*

*- Proverb from Sukuma, Tanzania*

## How to Contact the Author

**David S. Wu** welcomes and encourages communications from you. In the spirit of continuous improvement, Wu & Associates LLC is a Virginia, USA Company that provides consulting services including international trade and private publishing services. Working with partners, we also engage in executive searches and deliver diversity related consulting, training, and eLearning. Feel free to make contact with comments and ideas for future editions, or relevant topics. The Reader Feedback form is provided behind this page for this purpose.

**David S. Wu**
**President**
**Wu & Associates LLC**

Phone: 1-202-361-8081
Fax:     1-703-748-2176

Email: dswu@alumni.princeton.edu or david.wu.wg82@wharton.upenn.edu

Web site:  Http://members.cox.net/wuandassociatesllc

## Reader Feedback

### *"Organizing For Profit in China – A Case Study Approach"*

This book focuses on the practical aspects of Organizing for Profit in China. It touches upon the historical foundation of China's business culture through the thousands of years, and did not address the specific styles of the Chinese during negotiations.

Send the author a note commenting on the areas to improve upon this book, and areas you would be most interested in a more elaborate exchange. Beginning with emails, we could create an online community if that is appropriate.

__ Yes, I am interested in having David S. Wu speak or give a seminar to my company, association, school, or organization. Please send me information.
__ Yes, I am interested in joining the community, please include my information below
__ Yes, I am interested in a second book more focused on
        ____ History/Philosophy
        ____ Case Studies
        ____ Culture
        ____ Negotiations
        ____ Others (please specify_____)


Name_____

Organization_____

Address_____

City/State/Zip_____

Phone_____

Email_____

胡氏企業

Http://members.cox.net/wuandassociatesllc/home

Emails: dswu@alumni.princeton.edu; David.Wu.wg82@wharton.upenn.edu

Fax: 1-703-748-2176

*Remember:*

*What goes around comes around.*

*Work like you don't need the money.*

*Love like you've never been hurt.*

*Dance like nobody's watching.*

*Sing like nobody's listening.*

*Live like it's Heaven on Earth.*

0-595-26796-3